THE PRACTICAL WRITER

2nd edition

paragraph to theme

Edward P. Bailey, Jr.

Philip A. Powell

Jack M. Shuttleworth

Holt, Rinehart and Winston
New York   Chicago   San Francisco   Philadelphia
Montreal   Toronto   London   Sydney
Tokyo   Mexico City   Rio de Janeiro   Madrid

Library of Congress Cataloging in Publication Data

Bailey, Edward P., Jr.
  The practical writer.

  Includes index.
  1. English language—Rhetoric.   I. Powell, Philip A.
II. Shuttleworth, Jack M.   III. Title.
PE1408.B226 1982   808'.042   82-12121
ISBN 0-03-061739-1

CBS COLLEGE PUBLISHING
Holt, Rinehart and Winston
The Dryden Press
Saunders College Publishing

How This Book Works

This second edition of The Practical Writer, like the first, is intended for typical first-year college students, who lack knowledge but not intelligence. We assume that they know all too little about writing but that they can learn quickly and well from a step-by-step approach to the fundamentals, good examples for them to follow, and carefully designed exercises.

We begin by presenting the fundamentals (organization, support, unity, coherence)—one at a time—in a tightly structured one-paragraph essay. The paragraph, we've found, is a unit large enough for students to demonstrate their understanding of the fundamentals and small enough for them to work toward mastering. At this point, we don't overwhelm them while they're learning the fundamentals by making them struggle to find support; instead, we ask them to write about personal experiences and the people and things they know well. We encourage them to be colorful, interesting, and—above all—specific.

We then move through several longer stages of writing to a 1000-to-2000-word research paper. By the time students complete the research block, they can write a serious paper—the kind they will have to write in other college courses and beyond them—with a less mechanical structure than we required earlier. We still offer a model, of course, but it becomes a guide rather than a goal.

The last two topics of our book, punctuation and expression, are not part of the step-by-step approach. These chapters can be studied anytime, whenever your students are ready for them. They are not typical handbook material, though, because we've been careful to select only what first-year students need to learn, leaving out the skills they probably know and those they're not yet ready to apply.

Also, we try to avoid the "scholarly" style of writing and speak personally to the students, as though we're talking to them in class.

In this second edition of The Practical Writer we have kept the overall organization and much of the contents of the first edition. However, in the first four parts of the book we have changed examples and exercises to add variety and, more important, both to broaden the experience base represented and, in some cases, to demonstrate somewhat more sophisticated writing. In Part V, The Research Paper, we have rewritten portions to clarify instructions, in particular the chapter on note-taking to provide better explanations of types of notes and the reasons for taking them. For variety we also have changed exercises in the final two parts of the book.

Professor Paul Knoke deserves more credit than the acknowledgments section of a book can express. He read, analyzed, and fussed over every chapter in this book, spending the time and energy you would expect only from an author or publisher. Thanks, Paul. Your comments were invaluable.

We'd also like to thank our editors at Holt, especially Anne Boynton-Trigg, and Professor Richard S. Beal, whose insightful critiques contributed greatly to both editions of the book. Our gratitude is also extended to Michael J. Hogan, University of New Mexico; David Skwire, Cuyahoga Community College; David Martin, Monmouth College; David E. E. Sloane, University of New Haven; Becky Edgerton, University of Northern Colorado; Roger M. Haley, New Mexico State University; Pamela S. Rooney, Western Michigan University; Leon Guilhamet, the City College of the City University of New York; Anthony J. D'Angelo, Peirce Junior College; and Ronald G. Whitsitt, University of Southern Colorado.

Our students, of course, deserve special recognition. We admire their talent and creativity. We especially thank those students who contributed sample paragraphs and themes: Andrea M. Bopp, Louise A. Burket, Anthony J. Comtois, Robert T. Cunningham, Erik A. Emaus, George M. Fox, James C. Gall, James E. Kinzer, Janet C. Libby, Rodney L. Marshall, Jay D. McFadyen, Susan J. Timmons, Rodney R. Williams, and Lawrence A. Wolf.

November 1982
Iowa City, Iowa   Edward P. Bailey, Jr.
Burke, Virginia   Philip A. Powell
USAF Academy, Colorado   Jack M. Shuttleworth

Contents

PART V: THE RESEARCH PAPER   125

SECTION THREE: IMPROVING YOUR PUNCTUATION AND EXPRESSION

PART VI: PUNCTUATION   191

PART VII: EXPRESSION   223

THE PRACTICAL WRITER
Paragraph to Theme

section ONE

a model for writing

THE ONE-PARAGRAPH ESSAY (STAGE I)

This section teaches you how to write a good one-paragraph essay. Though you rarely see one-paragraph essays in publications, you'll find them remarkably handy for improving your writing. One obvious advantage is that they are short enough to allow you to spend your study time writing a really good one. Yet they are long enough for you to practice and demonstrate the fundamentals of writing. A final advantage is that what you learn about one-paragraph essays transfers nicely to larger themes and research papers.

Part I presents a very tightly structured model for a paragraph. You may wonder if all good writers follow such a structure for persuasive writing. No, of course not. This structure is not *the* good way to write a paragraph, but it is *one* good way. And this way has a very real advantage: it automatically gives your paper organization so that you have one less thing to worry about. You can then concentrate on learning the other fundamentals that experienced writers already know. And by working constantly with this model paragraph, you will learn organization too— the easy way.

Support for the paragraph's main idea is also easy. Right now we don't care if you know how to find facts in the library. We're much more concerned that you can recognize and use good support once you find it. So we make finding it simple. You don't need to go any further than your own mind: you can use either your experiences or your imagination for support. As a result, you can have fun with your one-paragraph essays. They can be intriguing and perhaps humorous. Writing doesn't have to be dull!

CHAPTER 1

Overview of the One-Paragraph Essay (Stage I)

You may already be familiar with the general organization of most good writing: tell the readers what you are going to tell them, tell it to them, then tell them what you have told them. This chapter shows you how to apply that organization to the one-paragraph essay: the first sentence states the idea you wish to persuade your readers to accept (we call this a *topic sentence*), all middle sentences present specific support, and the last sentence rewords the topic sentence to remind your readers of the point you have just made. The model for the one-paragraph essay looks like this:

> **Topic Sentence**
> > **Specific Support**
> > **Specific Support**
> > **Specific Support**
> **Reworded Topic Sentence**

Here is a sample one-paragraph essay:

Topic Sentence   The Boundary Waters Canoe Area, a wilderness park in northern Minnesota, is a refreshing change from the city. Away from the din of civilization, I have canoed silently across

Specific Support   its waters for an entire afternoon and not heard a single noise except an occasional birdcall and the sound of waves beating against the shore.

Specific Support   Also, my partner and I were able to navigate our way through a string of five lakes merely by following a single campfire's scent drifting through the pure air. Most refreshing, the park

Specific Support   is so magnificently beautiful that even the voyageurs of old were willing to endure its hardships in order to settle there. The Boundary

Reworded Topic Sentence   Waters Canoe Area is thus an ideal place to clear your head of the congestion of urban life.

Now look at an outline of the paragraph:

> **Topic Sentence:** The Boundary Waters Canoe Area is a refreshing change
> > **Specific Support:** Quietness
> > **Specific Support:** Purity of the air
> > **Specific Support:** Beauty
> **Reworded Topic Sentence:** Ideal place to clear head of congestion of urban life

Here's another sample one-paragraph essay:

Topic Sentence   Even though I have never really lived there, going to my grandmother's farm always seems like coming home. The feeling begins as soon as

Specific Support   I cross the threshold of that quaint little house and tumble into the arms of waiting aunts and cousins. The sense of welcome overwhelms me.

Specific Support   Then there are the cozy rooms—the ceilings are no higher than six feet—with their crackling fireplaces that make me want to snuggle down into the feather-stuffed chairs. But the memory

Specific Support   that always lasts the longest is the smell of Grandma's biscuits and pastries cooking in her coke-fed stove. Yes, only in Grandma's house do

Reworded Topic Sentence   I feel the warmth and welcome that always seems like coming home.

Again, let's outline it:

> **Topic Sentence:** Going to my grandmother's farm seems like coming home.
> > **Specific Support:** Greeting by relatives

  Specific Support: Coziness of house
  Specific Support: Smell of home-cooked food
 Reworded Topic Sentence: Visiting Grandma's seems like coming home.

  Notice that each of these sample paragraphs has three items of specific support. Sometimes five or six items are necessary to be convincing; other times one long example will do. As a general rule, though, three items seem to work well.

  The sample paragraphs in the first two or three chapters, though good, are intentionally fairly simple so that you can easily see the basic organization. But if you don't fully understand the one-paragraph essay yet, don't worry. The rest of Part I will explain the fundamentals. You can find a checklist for these fundamentals on page 55.

EXERCISES

A. Outline the following paragraph as the examples on p. 6 were outlined.

  Three common electric distractions on my desk waste my precious study time at night. The most notorious of these distractions is the clock, constantly humming to remind me how little time I actually have. Another interruption in the course of an evening of study comes when the high-quality fluorescent desk lamp begins to buzz, flicker, and eventually go out. And, finally, consider that fascinating little box, the calculator, that does all kinds of complicated math problems and even spells out simple words if I hold it upside down. After stopping to worry about the time, fix my lamp, and play with my calculator, I am too tired to study, so I just go to bed.

Topic Sentence: _____

_____

  Specific Support: _____

  Specific Support: _____

  Specific Support: _____

Reworded Topic Sentence: _____

_____

B. Outline this paragraph.

Old, stiff, and weathered, my grandfather's hands mirror the strenuous way of life he has known as a working man. Many hot summer days spent tilling the stubborn soil of West Texas have left their lasting mark in the form of a deep and permanent tan. Grandpa's hands are also covered with calluses—begun, perhaps, when he split cordwood for two dollars a day in an effort to pull his family through the Great Depression. Most striking, though, are the carpenter's scars he has collected from the days of building his house, barn, and fence, and from unending repair jobs that still occupy his every day. Although only in a small way, Grandpa's hands bring back images of a time when man worked from dawn to dusk just to survive, a simple but respected way of life.

Topic Sentence: _____

_____

     Specific Support: _____

     Specific Support: _____

     Specific Support: _____

Reworded Topic Sentence: _____

_____

C. Outline this paragraph.

The East Wing of the National Art Gallery in Washington, D.C., is a showplace of modern art. Inside, it houses collections of such artists as Picasso and Matisse, artists well known for their nonrepresentational works. Hanging from the ceiling is a mobile, normally thought of as a dangling toy parents hang above their infant's crib. This one, however, is several stories high and much more impressive to the parents. Even the building is in keeping with its contents—it has lots of glass, open spaces, and strange angles and corners. For modern art, then, this wing of the gallery is an excellent place to visit.

Topic Sentence: _____

_____

     Specific Support: _____

Specific Support: _____

Specific Support: _____

Reworded Topic Sentence: _____

_____

CHAPTER 2

Support: Examples, Statistics, Statements by Authorities

The first sentence in our model paragraph is the topic sentence, but let's save discussing that for the next chapter. We'll start instead with support. Once you understand support—and how specific it must be—you'll understand much more easily how to write a good topic sentence.

This chapter presents three different kinds of support: *examples, statistics,* and *statements by authorities.*

EXAMPLES

You know what an example is. It's one instance, one occurrence, of whatever you're talking about. If you're talking about the meals available at fast-food chain restaurants, a hamburger is one example—one of several possibilities. You could have named fried chicken, or hot dogs, or many other foods. Sometimes a simple example like this will serve very well to illustrate your idea. At other times, you'll want something more elaborate. If you're talking about the advantages of vegetarianism, you may want to tell us in a few sentences the remarkable story of your cousin Roger and how much healthier he is now that he eats only sunflower seeds. Examples, then, can cover a wide range. They extend from a specific item or instance (hamburgers) to a brief story (Roger's vegetarian diet).

For an example to be effective, it must be very specific. If you want to show that Sharon Gaston can't stick with anything, don't just say "she changes her mind a lot." Don't even just say "she changed her major frequently in college." Be still more specific: *"she changed her major from philosophy to biology and then to animal husbandry—all in one semester."*

If you want to show that shark-hunting is dangerous, don't just say "a friend of mine was once maimed while hunting sharks." Give us the details: "I still have nightmares about the time last June when Rocky and I were scuba diving off the coast of Baja California. Rocky spotted a great white shark and tried to shoot it with his spear gun. As he fired, the shark spun suddenly toward him. Before I knew what happened...." Then (poor Rocky) finish the story.

See the difference? The details make your writing interesting and much more convincing than bland generalities.

You may have noticed that the details about Rocky form the second type of example, the brief story or narrative that illustrates your main idea. Because the narrative can be such vivid and compelling evidence, let's examine it more closely.

The narrative example is a specific incident (with names, dates, and other details) that helps prove your point. The well-written popular magazines are filled with them. In an article in *Time* or *Newsweek* about high blood pressure, we might find a narrative example like this:

> Sally Rockwell, a twenty-three-year-old graduate student in architecture at the University of Colorado, had a blood pressure of 180/120 in February 1978. Her doctor prescribed Elavil, which Sally took regularly for three months until she became so busy with exams that she found taking medicine too much trouble. After exams, she still neglected her medicine. As a result, her blood pressure rose so sharply that in September she was rushed to the hospital with a stroke.

Do we care that this patient was an architecture student, or that she was twenty-three, or that she was named Sally Rockwell? Yes, somehow we do. Sally becomes more real to us, someone we can sympathize with, and because Sally's case seems believable and typical, we begin to be convinced that people with high blood pressure should take their medicine. The narrative example has helped convince us.

Now let's apply what we've learned to the one-paragraph essay. Suppose you are sitting in your room trying to write your first college English paper—the one for this course. You remember your professor's words: "I want to see examples—specific examples—and at least three of them!" He's told you to write about something that distracts you. You look aimlessly around the room, your eyes suddenly brighten, and you slap down this sentence:

My roommate distracts me when I try to study.

Then you think of some examples. Let's see—she has that record player going again, she's smacking her gum as usual, and you remember all those dumb questions she asks every few minutes. Here goes:

> Although my roommate is a helpful companion at times, she is a distracting nuisance whenever I try to study. Throughout the evening, her stereo blares in my ears. Even worse, she also insists on smacking her gum. She also interrupts me with questions that have nothing to do with homework. At any other time my roommate is a friend, but while I'm studying, she is my greatest enemy.

"Pretty good," you say. "I think I'll show it to my roommate to see what she— On second thought. . . ."

Now, suppose you're sitting in your room a couple of days later, ego deflated by a bad grade, trying to *rewrite* that paper. Your examples seemed specific enough to you—record player, gum, questions—but they obviously weren't. How could you have been more specific?

Instead of presenting the *kinds* of things your roommate does to distract you, you could have talked about one specific study period. Then you could have told us what record she was playing, what kind of gum she was chewing, what dumb questions she asked. In other words, you could have written this paragraph:

> Although my roommate is a helpful companion at times, she is a distracting nuisance whenever I try to study. Just last Wednesday night, Anna decided to spend the evening playing her old Bob Dylan records. While I was trying to figure out how to integrate a math function, all I could hear was Dylan complaining that the answer was somewhere in the wind. Even worse, the entire time Dylan was rasping away, Anna accompanied him by smacking and popping her Bazooka bubble gum. I'd finally given up on math and started my struggle with chemistry when she abruptly asked (loudly, of course, so I could hear her over the music), "Do you think any Cokes are left in the Coke machine?" My stomach started rumbling and my throat suddenly felt dry—even drier than the chem book I was reading. As I dropped a quarter into the Coke machine, I realized that although Anna is usually a friend, while I'm studying she is my greatest enemy.

We can now picture you, Anna, and all those distractions. Those details —even the Bazooka bubble gum—help make your writing colorful and convincing.

Before leaving the example, let's look at the writing of an expert. Erma Bombeck wrote the following article about Christmas toys. It's not a one-paragraph essay, of course, but it does illustrate the effectiveness of detailed support:

Indestructible Toys Never Had a Chance

If you are like millions of average parents you are sitting there today in the midst of toys that are solid, childproof, indestructible and built-to-be-abused.

A wheel has fallen off the Last-A-Lifetime car. The mend-itself, puncture-proof inflatable ball didn't and wasn't. The reinforced heavy-duty cardboard castle with 280 lifelike warriors, 38 weapons and 180-piece cavalry blew over when the furnace went on, and one of the kids has swallowed a one-piece durable, no-moving-parts barnyard guaranteed safe for toddlers.

You are naive if you believe there is any such toy as one that is "child-proof." I have seen sweet, shy precious little girls who did not have the strength to put their arm in a coat punch out the eyes of a doll and within minutes have her insides stacked neatly into three piles.

I have seen little boys small enough to walk under a coffee table pull a jungle gym set out of the ground and tie the swings into square knots.

Somehow, I've always identified with the commercial where they put a suitcase in a cage with a gorilla to see how sturdy the luggage stands up. Two minutes with my middle child and it wouldn't stand a chance. For that matter, neither would the luggage.

My mother once bought our children a Music Forever phonograph, touted to transcend those "terrible toys." It was like waving a flag in front of Attila the Hun. Within minutes, they were whining, "Grandma, the needle is bent." (An occasion marked by my mother's famous observation, "Don't ever turn your back on them!")

When you think about it, most toys don't die from old age. In fact, most of the dolls I have discarded have fear in their eyes. (Also hair torn out by the roots, dislocated joints and teethmarks on 95 percent of their bodies.)

Do not be misled by children who feign helplessness at not being able to get a bandaid out of the wrapper. Have you ever seen them tear into a package of gum? It's enough to make your blood run cold.

To my knowledge, we only owned one toy that lasted longer than 15 minutes. It was a robot monster that ran on batteries and held me at bay in the sink for eight hours with a laser gun pointed at my head.

Now that I think of it...it was probably running for its life from the children.*

Remove the examples from the above essay and what is left?

STATISTICS

Examples are an important form of evidence. They help convince your reader and make the essay more interesting. Examples alone, though, may not be enough. We need something else; we need some numbers. Who doesn't love numbers, trust them, believe in them? Give an American a statistic he does not suspect is phony, and he is probably convinced right there. Sally Rockwell and her trouble with high blood pressure may move him emotionally, but he will more likely be persuaded by a medical report like this:

> Recent statistics show convincingly that jogging is saving the lives of many Americans. Of the 2.5 million who jog at least 10 miles a week, 78% have a pulse rate and blood pressure lower than non-joggers their same age have. Estimates indicate that these joggers can expect to live to an average age of 75—more than three years longer than the average age of their contemporaries. The lesson seems clear, doesn't it?

To be convincing, statistics must be unambiguous. We are not necessarily alarmed, for example, to hear that 47 of 54 football players were injured in a practice session because we have no way of knowing how serious the injuries were. Perhaps 46 of the players were treated with Band-aids. We would become alarmed, however, to hear that 47 of 54 football players were hospitalized for at least one night following a practice session. The second statistic defines *injury* more clearly, so it is more convincing than the first.

STATEMENTS BY AUTHORITIES

The last kind of evidence we will consider in this chapter is the statement by an authority, a person who is in a position to know about something. If someone we trust tells us something, we just might believe him. But we do so because we trust *him:* his character, his judgment, and his knowledge of the subject. We would never believe Sally Rockwell, the ar-

---

* From *At Wit's End* by Erma Bombeck. Copyright © 1976 Field Enterprises, Inc. Courtesy of Field Newspaper Syndicate.

chitecture student who forgot to take her pills, if she tells us that shark-hunting is one of the safest sports, but we might listen to her if she tells us that patients with high blood pressure should take their medicine. We might also believe the president of the American Medical Association or a research specialist in high blood pressure or our family doctor—people who know what they're talking about.

Who are some people whose unsupported opinions about high blood pressure would not be convincing? We would not trust someone whose character, judgment, or knowledge of the subject is questionable. We would not trust the unsupported opinion of the druggist convicted of selling overpriced drugs to people who did not need them anyway; we would not trust the doctor being investigated for gross incompetence by the American Medical Association; and we would not trust our roommate, who thinks blood pressure is measured by a thermometer. The first has doubtful character; the second, doubtful judgment; and the third, doubtful knowledge.

By the way, the use of authority is particularly important when you are presenting statistics. Remember all those impressive figures about people who jog? Guess where the numbers came from. For all you know (and, in fact, for all those statistics are worth), they came from Miss Fisher's sixth-grade creative writing class. The point, of course, is that unless the writer tells you the source of his statistics, you don't know whether or not you should trust them.

Here's a revision of that paragraph showing the use of authorities, both with and without statistics:

> Recent statistics show convincingly that jogging is saving the lives of many Americans. According to the Congressional Subcommittee on Physical Fitness, 78% of the 2.5 million people who jog at least 10 miles per week have a pulse rate and blood pressure lower than non-joggers their same age have. This committee estimates that these joggers can expect to live to an average age of 75—more than three years longer than the average age of their contemporaries. Dr. Hans Corpuscle, chief advisor to the committee, says that "joggers are the healthiest single group of people in America today." The lesson seems clear, doesn't it?

COMBINED TYPES OF SUPPORT

A paragraph that uses one type of support—examples, maybe—is often convincing, but many good paragraphs contain several types: a couple of examples and some statistics, or a statement by an authority and an example, and so on.

The following paragraph attempts to prove that people attend yard sales for entertainment. Can you identify the types of support?

> Although you might think that most people attend yard sales for the bargains, the main reason they attend is for the entertainment they find there. For example, consider what happened to my family last summer when we held a yard sale to get rid of some old things before moving to a new place. Many people came, but few bought. Each new carload of people disgorged a new group that would while away an hour or so on a Saturday by caressing the sun-faded curtains, thumbing through ancient *National Geographic* magazines, and carefully considering sweaters eight sizes too small for them or anyone else in their group. Then the group would gather around a folded section of the classified ads and pick the next sale they'd visit. My suspicions about why those people came to our sale were confirmed a few months later by a survey I read in *Psychology Monthly*. That survey showed that seven of ten people who attended yard sales admitted that they did so "just for the fun of it." The psychologist who conducted the survey then reached a conclusion I could have told him last summer: "The real bargain that people seek at yard sales, if only subconsciously, is not another frying pan or partially burned plastic spatula, but just a little weekend entertainment."

Notice that the statement by the authority is an effective rewording of the topic sentence, so no separate concluding sentence is necessary for this paragraph.

The above paragraph uses all three kinds of evidence—all of it invented by the writer. When you are inventing evidence for exercises or when you find it in books or magazines, statistics and statements by authorities are no problem. If, however, you are writing paragraphs based on personal experiences (much like many samples in Section I), you will naturally rely heavily on examples. Fortunately, the example is one of the most colorful and convincing kinds of evidence.

INVENTED EVIDENCE

Before you begin the exercises, let's have a word about invented evidence. It greatly simplifies the learning process for you. You don't have to struggle to locate real evidence at the same time you are trying to figure out just what good evidence is. You don't have to search any further than your own mind, and you can be as specific as you like.

But remember, inventing evidence is just an exercise, a convenience for you and your instructor. *Never write invented evidence unless your readers will know that is what they are reading. Never write invented evidence unless your instructor approves.*

Within this guideline, you can have fun with your writing. Erma Bombeck's article "Indestructible Toys Never Had a Chance" certainly uses invented evidence—we all know that. Try to be as imaginative as she is. At the same time, be realistic. Don't, for instance, try to convince us that the Grand Junction School of Cosmetology is noted for its scholarly excellence because it had thirteen Rhodes Scholars last year. The school may be good, but such a ridiculous figure is bound to raise eyebrows.

EXERCISES

A. For each of the topic sentences below, invent (in other words, simply make up evidence) a narrative example (3–5 sentences long), a statistic (1–2 sentences long), and a statement by an appropriate authority (1–2 sentences long), as required. Use the sample paragraph on yard sales, which has invented evidence, as a model.

1. TV video games are a waste of time.

   a. Example: _____

_____

_____

_____

_____

_____

   b. Statistic: _____

_____

_____

   c. Statement by an authority: _____

_____

_____

2. Railroads are an excellent way to transport perishable agricultural products over long distances.

   a. Statement by an authority: _____

_____

_____

   b. Example: _____

_____

_____

_____

_____

   c. Statistic: _____

_____

3. Flying is dangerous.
   a. Statistic: _____

_____

   b. Example: _____

_____

_____

_____

_____

   c. Statement by an authority: _____

_____

_____

B. Follow the same instructions for these topic sentences.

  1. TV video games are more worthwhile than most people think.
     a. Statement by an authority: _____

_____

_____

    b.   Example: _____

_____

_____

_____

_____

_____

    c.   Example: _____

_____

_____

_____

_____

2.   Railroads are a poor way to transport perishable agricultural products over long distances.

    a.   Example: _____

_____

_____

_____

_____

    b.   Statistic: _____

_____

_____

    c.   Example: _____

_____

_____

_____

3.   Although many people believe otherwise, flying is safe.

    a.   Example: _____

_____

_____

_____

_____

_____

b. Statement by an authority: _____

_____

_____

c. Statement by an authority: _____

_____

_____

C. Look again in this chapter at Erma Bombeck's article, "Indestructible Toys Never Had a Chance." How would a weak writer—one who didn't know he should use detailed examples—have written the second paragraph? Like this, maybe?

> The toy car broke, the plastic ball didn't work, the castle blew over, and someone swallowed another one of the toys.

Dull and ineffective. Now you try to ruin a couple of paragraphs:

1. Rewrite the sixth paragraph of Erma Bombeck's article into one far-too-general sentence:

_____

_____

_____

_____

2. Look at the yard sales paragraph that ended this chapter. Rewrite the good example presented in the second through the fifth sentences by making it too general:

_____

_____

_____

_____

D. Now let's reverse Exercise C. Here are some topic sentences followed by an example that is too general. Improve the italicized example by converting the dull generalities into specific details. You'll need two or three sentences for each one.

1. Dieting is impossible for me. *Yesterday, for example, I ate a huge meal.*

_____

_____

_____

_____

_____

2. Routine inspection of bridges is important. *Sometimes older bridges collapse without warning.*

_____

_____

_____

_____

_____

3. The price of clothes is outrageous. *The clothes I just bought for school, for instance, were incredibly expensive.*

_____

_____

_____

_____

_____

E. In Exercises A and B above, you outlined six paragraphs. Select the one that interests you the most and use the evidence you invented to write the paragraph. The appendix (pages 271–273) gives you the proper format.

CHAPTER 3

Topic Sentence

Now we move to the first sentence of the one-paragraph essay, to its intellect—the thought at the head of the body. That thought, called the topic sentence, is the primary idea of the paragraph, the central idea you wish to persuade your reader to accept.

Writing texts attempt to define the topic-sentence idea with a number of terms: it is the writer's "viewpoint" of his topic, his "judgment" about the topic, his "conviction," his "assertion" of truth. Those texts are right; the topic-sentence idea is all these things. However, we prefer the term *opinion:* the topic sentence is a precise statement of opinion you wish to persuade your reader to accept.

Why do we associate a topic sentence with the word *opinion?* An opinion is a judgment that seems true only for the person who believes it. Imagine for a moment that you're telling a friend something you believe —a viewpoint, a judgment, a conviction, an assertion you hold to be true. Your friend replies "That's just your opinion." He's not denying that you believe what you say, but he is letting you know that you'll have to persuade him to agree with you. He's placing the burden on you to support your belief so that he can accept the idea as fully as you do. A similar relationship exists between you the writer and your readers. Your topic sentence stands as a statement of your opinion *until* you persuade your audience to accept it fully. Thus, recognizing that the topic sentence is a statement of opinion will help you remember your obligation to support your idea.

Why should the topic sentence be an opinion instead of a fact? If you state your idea and your reader responds with "Oh, yes, that's true" or "That's a fact," what more can you say? Suppose you write this topic sentence:

William Shakespeare wrote *Hamlet.*

In your paragraph you could discuss Shakespeare or his play, but you wouldn't be trying to convince a reader to accept the topic sentence itself. That Shakespeare wrote *Hamlet* is accepted as fact. And statements of fact (or at least what everyone accepts as fact) don't make good topic sentences because they leave the writer nothing important to say. On the other hand, suppose you try this topic sentence:

Francis Bacon wrote *Hamlet.*

Now you've stated an opinion. Unfortunately, hardly anyone believes it. You've crossed into such extreme controversy that you'll have to really work to convince a reader to accept your topic-sentence idea.

Your topic-sentence opinion doesn't need to arouse instant doubt. You don't need to take outrageous stands like these:

Dogs are really man's greatest enemy.

A toupee is better than real hair.

In fact, most topic sentences bring neither instant acceptance nor instant doubt. Usually readers have not formed their own judgments, and they're willing to accept yours if you persuade them. For example, consider this topic sentence:

Today's toupees are so well made that they look like a person's own hair.

The writer is stating what she believes to be fact. Although readers have no reason to doubt her, they are not obliged to believe her either. They will probably agree with what she says once she provides specific support for her opinion. And it *is* her opinion—until she persuades the audience to accept it as fully as she does.

When you write a one-paragraph essay, you'll begin with a topic sentence and follow it with specific support (examples, statistics, or authoritative statements). If you structure the topic sentence well and support it well with specifics, you'll persuade your readers to accept your idea fully. The rest of this chapter shows you how to write a good topic sentence.

A good topic sentence contains two parts: a *limited subject* and a *precise opinion* about that subject.

LIMITING THE SUBJECT

The first step in writing a good topic sentence is to select a subject limited enough to support in a single paragraph. If you attempt to support a large subject in a one-paragraph essay, your argument is not likely to be convincing because the subject (which is too general) will demand more support than you can develop in one paragraph. Thus, limiting the subject is the first step toward writing a good topic sentence.

Let's examine a sample case. You begin with a general subject, say advertising. Since the topic is obviously too large for a one-paragraph essay, you must limit it. Of the many types of advertisement (television, radio, newspaper, billboard, and the like), you choose one—for instance, magazine advertising. As you glance at the advertisements in your favorite magazine, three attract your attention. In one advertisement you see a scantily clad darling holding a tape recorder she wants you to buy. In another a shapely blonde is stroking a luxury automobile. And in a third ad a couple embrace in delight as they hold cigarettes in their free hands. You see a common element in each sales pitch: the advertisers use sex appeal to make you want the things you see before you. In this way you limit the subject from "advertising" to "magazine advertising" to "sex appeal in magazine advertising."

Consider the process you just went through. You might have noticed the lack of color in the tape-recorder advertisement, the large amount of space wasted in the automobile ad, or the small print that obscures the Surgeon General's warning in the cigarette advertisement. Instead you focused your attention on sex appeal in the ads, thereby limiting the subject.

STATING THE PRECISE OPINION

The second portion of the topic sentence provides precise definition to your opinion about the limited subject. Although limiting the subject is a step toward precision, an opinion about even a limited subject will remain vague unless you tell the reader what your idea is exactly.

The precise-opinion portion of the topic sentence is a word or phrase that makes a judgment, such as *dangerous* or *exciting.* But a warning is necessary here, for not all judgment words will express precise opinions. Words like *interesting, nice, good,* or *bad* start to take a stand but remain vague. What do you really mean when you say something is "interesting"? What have you said about a person you call "nice"? Such vague judgments make imprecise opinions. On the other hand, precise judgments combine with a subject to define your opinion about the subject.

Again, let's apply this theory to our sample case, the sex appeal in magazine advertising. So what if advertisers support sales with sex appeal? You look again at the ads that will support your argument only to find another common element: sex appeal isn't really related to the items for sale. The ads held your attention because sex appeal was connected to nonsexual items. You are irritated because the advertisers are trying to manipulate your senses so that you will buy whatever they put in the advertisements. Thus, you are ready to state precisely your opinion about sex appeal in these three advertisements: it irritates you.

Again consider the process you used. You had to make a judgment about sex appeal in the advertising; you had to establish your precise opinion about the subject. Because you didn't like the sex appeal in the ads, you might have said that the sex appeal was bad. But what would *bad* mean? Did the sex appeal disgust you? Did it appeal to your prurient interests in a manner not consistent with community standards (whatever that means)? Did the sex appeal in the ads merely irritate you? Just what was the "badness"? When you made the precise judgment that sex appeal in some magazine advertisements is irritating, you established your exact stand on the subject.

WRITING THE TOPIC SENTENCE

Once you have limited the subject and have decided precisely your opinion about it, you have formed the two basic parts of the topic sentence—a *limited subject* and a *precise opinion* about that subject. You can easily structure a topic sentence by stating the precise opinion in some form after the sentence's subject, as in the following:

> For me, dieting is futile.

Dieting, the subject of the sentence, is the limited subject, and *futile,* which follows, is the precise opinion about it.
Now we can write the topic sentence for the paragraph on sex appeal in magazine advertisements.

> Magazine advertisements that try to use sex appeal to sell any product are irritating.

> We can see, then, that the basic pattern for the topic sentence is *"limited subject* is *precise opinion."* Consider these examples:

> Arcade video games are challenging.

> Restoring old houses is rewarding.

In the first sentence, *arcade video games* is the limited subject and *challenging* is the precise opinion. In the second, you intend to persuade the reader that *restoring old houses* (the limited subject) is *rewarding* (the precise opinion).

REFINING THE TOPIC SENTENCE

Even though this pattern is basic for a topic sentence, you need not feel restricted to it. Perhaps the model seems too mechanical. You can easily convert the topic-sentence model to a more sophisticated form. Look at the following topic sentence in the basic pattern:

> Overpackaging of supermarket items is seriously wasteful of natural resources.

Here is the same idea in another form:

> The overpackaging of supermarket items seriously wastes natural resources.

Notice that the verb *is* and the precise opinion *wasteful* (the basic pattern) became the verb *wastes* in the second sentence form. Now look at a topic sentence from an earlier chapter:

> Even though I have never really lived there, going to my grandmother's farm always seems like coming home.

Converted to the basic pattern, the idea of the sentence is as follows:

> Going to my grandmother's farm is like coming home.

In another topic sentence we may say this:

> Hitchhiking is dangerous.

But we may also state the sentence more imaginatively:

> Hitchhiking has proved to be the last ride for many people.

The important point is that refined topic sentences, such as those above, can always be converted to the model: *"limited subject is precise opinion."* When you write a topic sentence form beyond the model, take a moment to insure that you can still convert it to the two basic parts.

Whatever the pattern of the topic sentence, the result is the same. When you have limited your subject and precisely defined your opinion about it, you have formed the necessary parts of the topic sentence. You have created an assertion that will guide both you and your reader through the supporting material of the paragraph. In one sentence you've taken a stand that you will then persuade your reader to believe. You've given form to the idea that rests at the head of the body.

EXERCISES

A. Place a check mark by the sentences that would *not* make good topic sentences because they do not state opinions:

_____ 1. Let me tell you about the parade.

_____ 2. Young children participating in parades usually look foolish.

_____ 3. According to the U.S. Weather Service, eight inches of snow fell overnight.

_____ 4. The snowfall turned the city streets into a nightmare for commuters.

_____ 5. The snowfall blanketed the city streets.

_____ 6. Van Gogh painted "The Starry Night."

_____ 7. Certain details in "The Starry Night" indicate Van Gogh's emotional disturbance.

_____ 8. "The Rocky Horror Picture Show" usually runs at midnight.

_____ 9. "The Rocky Horror Picture Show" invokes bizarre audience participation.

_____ 10. Doctors should be recertified every five years.

B. In the topic sentences below, underline the subject once and the opinion twice. In addition, circle any subjects that are not limited enough and any opinions that are not precise enough.

1. Nursing in an intensive care unit is rewarding.
2. Now that I haven't the time, sleep has become my most cherished possession.
3. Traveling is great.
4. The time machine was unreliable.
5. Pool halls are lousy.
6. Grooming a poodle is difficult.
7. Summer vacations are wonderful.
8. Associating with students from different backgrounds has made me more tolerant of other people's habits.
9. The most significant change I have noticed in myself recently is my ability to memorize material quickly.
10. When the pack is not on the back, backpacking is exhilarating.

C. Limit the general subjects below and then state a precise opinion about each limited subject:

Example: General Subject: Traveling

Hitchhiking	is/are	dangerous
(Limited Subject)		(Precise Opinion)

1. General Subject: Energy

_____	is/are	_____ .
(Limited Subject)		(Precise Opinion)

2. General Subject: Medicine

_____ is/are _____ .
      (Limited Subject)   (Precise Opinion)

3. General Subject: Clothing

_____ is/are _____ .
      (Limited Subject)   (Precise Opinion)

4. General Subject: Welfare

_____ is/are _____ .
      (Limited Subject)   (Precise Opinion)

5. General Subject: Computers

_____ is/are _____ .
      (Limited Subject)   (Precise Opinion)

6. General Subject: Censorship

_____ is/are _____ .
      (Limited Subject)   (Precise Opinion)

D.   In Exercise C above, you wrote six topic sentences in the basic pattern of *"limited subject* is *precise opinion."* Now convert any three of these sentences to another form with the same meaning.

Example: Hitchhiking has proved to be the last ride for many people.

1. _____

_____

2. _____

_____

3. _____

_____

E.   In Exercises C and D above, you wrote nine topic sentences. Select the one that interests you the most and use invented evidence to write the paragraph. Be sure you have the kind of specific support you learned about in Chapter 2.

CHAPTER 4

Unity

Now that you know a topic sentence presents a precise opinion about a limited subject, we can go to the next step in good writing: unity. For a paragraph to have unity, each of the supporting details—examples, statistics, or authoritative statements—must relate directly to the topic sentence. If you are writing about the dullest class you ever took, you destroy unity by praising the fascinating lectures and the exciting field trips. Or if you want to argue that your mynah bird is an ideal pet, the friendliness of the boa constrictor is off the subject and, therefore, irrelevant. In other words, everything you say in a paragraph must support the topic sentence.

Look at this paragraph:

> The most frustrating job I ever had was cooking for the dorm cafeteria during my freshman year. No matter how hard I tried, I never could cook what the menu said because the food company always delivered the wrong food or brought it late. The cafeteria supervisor was so mad he called up the company almost every day to complain. Another reason for my frustration was that I have trouble estimating the right amount of food. I'd always come up with three dozen hamburgers and only half a pound of French fries. The worst thing, though, was the condition of the kitchen floor. Even though I was careful, the floor was so slick I'd slip every time I moved from the grill to the counter and spill the spaghetti or soup, and just add to the mess. And then the other students were always complaining about their eight o'clock class or their exams or their profs; they were never happy. No wonder I thought being a cook for the dorm cafeteria was frustrating.

In this paragraph the writer loses the sense of unity by going off the subject. Not all the facts support the precise opinion of the topic sentence: cooking in the dorm cafeteria frustrated the writer. The writer was frustrated with his cooking job, but not because the cafeteria supervisor called the food company to complain or because the students were unhappy with college. Because not all the support here relates directly to the topic sentence, the paragraph loses its unity.

A diagram of the paragraph will show what we mean:

| **Topic Sentence** |
| My job as cook was frustrating |
| **Support** |
| Wrong food was delivered |

| **Support** |
| Supervisor |
| complained to |
| food supplier |

| **Support** |
| I had trouble estimating amounts |
| **Support** |
| Kitchen floor was mess |

| **Support** |
| Students were |
| unhappy about |
| classes, etc. |

| **Conclusion** |
| My job as cook was frustrating |

Now read this paragraph:

The most frustrating job I ever had was cooking at the dorm cafeteria during my freshman year. No matter how hard I tried, I never could cook what the menu said because the food company always delivered the wrong food or brought it late. Another reason for my frustration was that I have trouble estimating the right amount of food. I'd always come up with three dozen hamburgers and only half a pound of French fries. The worst thing, though, was the condition of the kitchen floor. Even though I was careful, the floor was so slick I'd slip every time I moved from the grill to the counter and spill the spaghetti or soup, and just add to the mess. No wonder I thought being a cook for the dorm cafeteria was frustrating.

Note the difference: here the writer has stuck to the subject. All the examples help show how being a cook for the dorm cafeteria was frustrating. A diagram of this paragraph looks unified; it shows how all the blocks fit:

Topic Sentence My job as cook was frustrating
Support Wrong food was delivered
Support I had trouble estimating amounts
Support Kitchen floor was mess
Conclusion My job as cook was frustrating

As you can see, the idea of unity is really fairly simple: stick to the point. Don't be led astray by a word or idea in one of your sentences the way the writer was in the first paragraph. The idea of the bad delivery service led to the idea of the supervisor's complaining, but his complaining doesn't support the precise idea of the topic sentence—that the cook was frustrated. The point of this chapter should be clear by now: make sure everything in your paragraph belongs there.

EXERCISES

A. Read the paragraphs below and underline the precise opinion in the topic sentence. Identify those sentences that don't help support that precise opinion.

1. ¹Television comedy shows are destroying American social values. ²The most obvious way is that they usually show the father or other male power figure as foolish, incompetent, or corrupt. ³The shows also make women only sex objects, bouncy but brainless. ⁴Likewise, people who are honest or hardworking are made to look stupid. ⁵Some of the "one-liners" in these shows are pretty good, though. ⁶It's clear that sit-coms are destroying America's values.
     The irrelevant sentence is _____.
2. ¹Barbara Walters, a successful television newscaster, has outstanding personal qualities. ²Most important, she has quick wit. ³She also interviews interesting people in high positions and sometimes ordinary people who make the programs understandable. ⁴Likewise, the material in her editorial is usually very effective. ⁵The

film clips are always exciting to watch, too. ⁶It's pretty clear that Barbara Walters is an exceptional person.

The irrelevant sentences are _____, _____, and _____.

3. ¹My brother Dave is a disaster as a driver. ²Last week he misjudged the distance when he roared into a gas station and hit a gas pump with his left front fender. ³Gas spewed out all over the ground before the pump jockey could get it turned off. ⁴The jockey went to school with me and told me all about it. ⁵Another time Dave was backing out of the parking lot at the football game when his foot slipped off the clutch pedal, and the car leaped backward, and hit the superintendent's new Porsche and crumpled its fender, grill, and two headlights. ⁶Finally, Dave was trying to drive and eat pizza at the same time once. ⁷He inhaled some of the chili pepper and sneezed. ⁸When he sneezed, he jerked the steering wheel to the right and sideswiped a parked green Ford pick-up. ⁹The pizza flew out of his hand, landed in my lap, and ruined a new white skirt I had on. ¹⁰My dad had bought me the skirt for my birthday to go with my blue cashmere. ¹¹Frankly, I'm not a very good driver either, but I've had only two accidents. ¹²But sometimes Dave is a good driver; he made it from Boston to Cincinnati without any problems. ¹³Because of Dave's driving problems, I always take money along in case I have to take a taxi home or call for help.

a. The irrelevant sentences are _____, _____, _____, and

_____.

b. Why are sentences 3 and 9 unified with the topic sentence?

B. In the following examples, provide unified support for the topic sentence. If you need to, invent specific details for your support.

1.

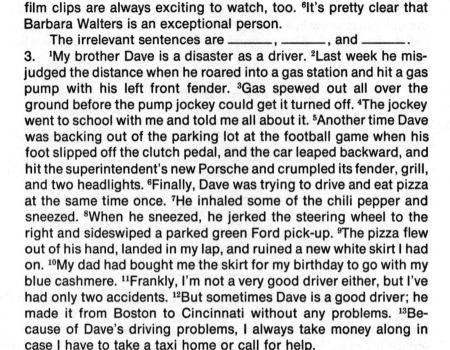

| **Topic Sentence**
Student loans are crucial. |
| **Support** |
| **Support** |
| **Support** |
| **Conclusion**
We need student loans. |

2.

Topic Sentence Cities need federal aid for mass transit.
Support
Support
Support
Conclusion Cities need federal aid for mass transit.

3.

Topic Sentence Cigarette smoking is destructive.
Support
Support
Support
Conclusion Cigarette smoking is destructive.

C. 1. Write a paragraph on one of the topic sentences in exercise B; use your invented support. Add two irrelevant sentences to destroy the paragraph's unity.

2. Now write the same paragraph but eliminate the irrelevant sentences so that your paragraph is unified.

CHAPTER 5

Coherence

A one-paragraph essay must have not only unity but also coherence, a word few students can define, though nearly everyone can recognize the opposite, incoherence. If a man runs into the room screaming "Fire! Dog! House!" we call him incoherent. Does he mean that a dog is on fire in the house? Or that the house is on fire with the dog inside? Or that a dog-house is on fire? We don't know. Although the man apparently has some very important ideas he wishes desperately to communicate, he has left out the essential links of thought. Coherence, then, requires including those links.

This chapter discusses three important ways to achieve coherence in the one-paragraph essay: *explanation of the support, reminders of the opinion in the topic sentence,* and *transitions.* These important links will help your reader move smoothly from idea to idea within your paragraph. Then when your doghouse catches on fire, you will know exactly how to ask for help.

EXPLANATION OF THE SUPPORT

Don't assume that your reader is a specially gifted person able to read minds. You must not only present the support to the reader but also explain how it is related to the topic sentence. In other words, you must link your support—clearly and unambiguously—to the topic sentence. The author of the following paragraph does not explain his support at all, apparently hoping that his reader is clairvoyant:

> In the early morning, I am easily annoyed by my roommate. I have to shut the ice-covered windows. A white tornado of dandruff swirls around the room. A mass of smoke from cigarettes hovers near the door. No wonder I find my roommate annoying!

No wonder, indeed! The paragraph is incoherent because the author has failed to explain how his support relates to the topic sentence. Does he mean that his roommate is annoying because he does not close the window in the morning? Or is he annoying because he opens the window every night, even in winter, thus causing the writer to be cold in the morning? Or what? And who has dandruff, and who smokes? Is it the roommate or is it the author, who is upset because the roommate does not understand? After all, the author may be doing the best he can to get rid of the dandruff, and he is smoking heavily only because he is trying to distract himself after waking up every morning in a cold room.

By being incomplete, by not explaining the support fully, the paragraph demands too much of the reader. Let's guess what the writer really meant and then revise the paragraph to add coherence:

Joh.

> In the early morning, I am easily annoyed by my roommate. I have to shut the ice-covered windows *which John, my roommate, insists on opening every night, even during the winter.* A white tornado swirling around the room *shows me that his dandruff problem is still in full force.* A mass of smoke *from John's pack-a-day habit* hovers near the door. No wonder I find my roommate annoying.

We have now explained that John, the roommate, is guilty of the indiscretions. The coherence is improved greatly, but the paragraph still needs work.

REMINDERS OF THE OPINION IN THE TOPIC SENTENCE

In the preceding section we learned not to assume that readers can read minds. In this section, however, we will make an assumption about readers: readers, like all of us, prefer being mentally lazy. They don't like remembering too much at once. While they are reading the support, they like occasional reminders of the opinion stated in the topic sentence so that they will remember why they are reading that support. We can remind them of the opinion in the topic sentence with either of two techniques at the beginning of each item of support: we can repeat the exact words of the opinion or use other words that suggest the opinion. In the sample paragraph about the roommate, we can use the word *annoy* in presenting each example, or we can use words such as *disgusted* or *choking on stale smoke*, both of which suggest annoyance. Notice the reminders in the revised paragraph:

Joh.

> In the early morning, I am easily annoyed by my roommate. *I am annoyed* each time I have to shut the ice-covered windows which John, my roommate, insists on opening every night, even during the winter. *A disgusting* white tornado swirling around the room shows me that his dandruff problem is still in full force. A

He has a severe case of dandruff.

choking mass of *stale* smoke from John's pack-a-day habit hovers near the door. No wonder I find my roommate annoying.

By reminding the readers that each example presents something annoying, the paragraph becomes more coherent.

TRANSITIONS

Each example in the sample paragraph now has a clear explanation of the support and a reminder of the opinion in the topic sentence, but the paragraph is still rough. It moves like a train with square wheels, chunking along abruptly from idea to idea. To help the paragraph move more smoothly, we must add transitions.

Transitions are like road signs which tell readers where they are going. If you live in Louisville and wish to drive north to Indianapolis, you don't want to stop to consult a map to find out you are on the right road. You would rather have road signs. Similarly, readers don't want to run into an example that slows them because they don't understand how it relates to the previous example or, worse yet, how it relates to the topic sentence. In a paragraph, the road sign could be *however* to tell readers that the next idea is going to contrast with the one just presented; or it could be *also* to tell readers that another idea like the preceding one is about to be presented; or it could be *therefore* to tell readers to prepare for a conclusion. These and other transitions will keep your Indianapolis-bound driver from losing valuable time because he has to stop, or, if he takes a chance and presses on, from arriving nowhere, which is where he may end his trip in a paragraph without transitions.

Here are some common transitions:

To add an idea: also, and, another, equally important, finally, furthermore, in addition, last, likewise, moreover, most important, next, second, third

To give an example: as a case in point, consider . . . , for example, for instance, as an illustration

To make a contrast: and yet, but, however, instead, nevertheless, on the contrary, on the other hand, still

To begin a conclusion: as a result, clearly, hence, in conclusion, no wonder, obviously, then, therefore, thus

A paragraph must have transitions, but where should these transitions be placed? This diagram shows the critical locations:

Topic Sentence

transition ──────────→

Specific Support

transition ──────────→

Specific Support

transition ──────────→

Specific Support

transition ──────────→

Reworded Topic Sentence

Sometimes you will find that no transition is necessary between the topic sentence and the first item of specific support because the second sentence of the paragraph is so obviously an example that a transitional expression seems too mechanical. For instance, you might be able to omit the first transition in this final revision of the sample paragraph about the roommate. The remaining transitions, however, are all desirable.

> In the early morning, I am easily annoyed by my roommate. *For example,* I am annoyed each time I have to shut the ice-covered windows which John, my roommate, insists on opening every night, even during the winter. I am *also* disgusted by a white tornado swirling around the room which shows me that his dandruff problem is still in full force. *Most bothersome, though,* is the choking mass of stale smoke—from John's pack-a-day habit—which hovers near the door. *No wonder* I find my roommate annoying.

Our sample paragraph is finally coherent. We have explained the support, reminded the reader frequently of the opinion in the topic sentence, and added transitions at the critical locations.

You're so familiar with the above paragraph by now, and it's so simple, you may believe the transitions aren't really necessary. Perhaps you're right. But what if you read a paragraph that began like this?

> If you've ever bought a pomegranate, you probably know that it's one of the most difficult foods to eat. The juice is delicious and a beautiful ruby color. It drips everywhere, staining whatever it hits. The bitter, inedible pulp seems impossible to avoid. . . .

By now, you're probably lost. If the writer has trouble eating a pomegranate, then why does he start by telling us how delicious and beautiful it is? The writer knows why, but the reader doesn't because there aren't any transitions. Let's put them in:

> If you've ever bought a pomegranate, you probably know that it's one of the most difficult foods to eat. *Although* the juice is delicious

and a beautiful ruby color, it *unfortunately* drips everywhere, staining whatever it hits. *Also frustrating,* the bitter, inedible pulp seems impossible to avoid....

The transitions (and the reminder *frustrating*) make the paragraph easy to understand the first time through. Good writing shouldn't be an IQ test or a guessing game for the reader, so let him know what you're thinking as your ideas shift directions. For now, use the three techniques demonstrated in this chapter, even if they seem mechanical. As you gain experience as a writer, you will learn more subtle ways to link your ideas to each other and to the topic sentence. Your immediate goal now, though, is to communicate coherently with your reader.

EXERCISES

A. Outline this paragraph and indicate the *transitions* by filling in the blanks below. Merely summarize the topic sentence, the support, and the reworded topic sentence rather than writing them in full.

> A significant change I have noticed in myself since entering college is a fear of mathematics. The mere sight of a three-hundred-fifty-page math text, for instance, causes a cold shiver to run the length of my spine. As I cautiously open the front cover of the text, a myriad of complex formulas springs at me, quickly eliminating any trace of confidence I may have had. My dread of math is also strengthened each time I enter the small, dismal classroom. I can find no consolation in watching my classmates cringe behind open briefcases as they prepare to do battle with a common enemy capable of engulfing us all in a blanket of confusion. Finally, my greatest fears are realized as my instructor self-consciously adjusts his glasses and admits that he majored in English and never truly mastered, or even understood, calculus. Then I suddenly realize that the cartesian plane has snared me in its nightmarish world for another semester.

| | Topic Sentence _____ |
| transition _____ |
| | Specific Support _____ |
| transition _____ |
| | Specific Support _____ |
| transition _____ |

Specific Support _____

transition _____

Reworded Topic Sentence _____

The opinion the above paragraph proves is *fear*. Circle all *reminders* of that opinion in the paragraph; that is, circle all words which either repeat the word or suggest the meaning *fear*.

B.   Outline this paragraph and indicate the *transitions* by filling in the blanks below. Again, merely summarize the topic sentence, the support, and the reworded topic sentence rather than writing them in full.

> Since becoming a college student, I have learned many methods that enable me to study faster than I ever did in high school. As an example, I discovered that spending three-fourths of my allotted study time sprawled across a desk in deep slumber has helped me find a sudden aptitude for instant memorization the period before a 1000-point chemistry test. Another well-developed study-skill builder in which I participate is the practice of reading magazines at the bookstore on free afternoons. When asked to justify this practice, I calmly express my belief that the rate at which I study is sure to increase if I work only in the evenings. But by far the most useful device I have encountered for sharpening my study habits is the custom of writing my girlfriend during finals week. What else could teach me to study an entire semester's material in only an hour and a half? Hence, since becoming a college student, I have acquired many methods which allow me to study far faster than I ever had before.

Topic Sentence _____

transition _____

Specific Support _____

transition _____

Specific Support _____

transition _____

Specific Support _____

transition _____

Reworded Topic Sentence _____

The opinion the above paragraph proves is *study faster*. Circle all *re-*

minders of that opinion in the paragraph; that is, circle all words which either repeat the word or suggest the meaning *study faster.*

C.   Using another paragraph in this book assigned by your instructor, underline all the transitions and circle all the reminders.

D.   Rewrite this paragraph, adding transitions and reminders of the opinion in the topic sentence. You may also need to add some support in order to explain fully the relationship of the support to the topic sentence.

> The city of Stockholm is among the loveliest in the world. Slum districts, prevalent in almost all large cities, are nearly nonexistent in Stockholm, having been replaced by government housing. The citizens are careful to dispose of their litter properly and to pick up litter other people may have dropped. Stockholm has a unique layout: it is built on twenty-three islands. Water winds throughout the city. The beauty of Stockholm makes it one of the most alluring cities in the world.

E.   Using one of the topic sentences you outlined for Exercises A and B in Chapter 2, and using invented evidence, write a paragraph. On the final copy, underline all the transitions and circle all the reminders. Insure you have met the other requirement for coherence by explaining your support fully.

F.   Write a paragraph that convinces the reader that some*thing* (not some*one*) has a particular characteristic. On the final copy, underline all the transitions and circle all the reminders. Insure you have met the other requirement for coherence by explaining your support fully. (Notice that the paragraph in Chapter 1 on the Boundary Waters Canoe Area could have been a response to this exercise.)

G.   Write a paragraph that convinces the reader of one significant way in which you have changed since entering college. Use examples from your own experience as support. On the final copy, underline all the transitions and circle all the reminders. Insure you have met the other requirement for coherence by explaining your support fully. (Notice that Exercises A and B in this section are on the same subject that this exercise assigns.)

PART II

THE ONE-PARAGRAPH ESSAY (STAGE II)

In this section you'll learn a slightly more sophisticated way to organize a one-paragraph essay. You'll find out when you reach Part III that this new type of paragraph is actually a stepping-stone to larger themes and research papers. Once you learn how to write a Stage II paragraph, the full-length essay will be simple for you to learn.

CHAPTER 6

Overview of the One-Paragraph Essay (Stage II)

Good Stage I and Stage II paragraphs have much in common: a topic sentence, specific support, unity, coherence, and a reworded topic sentence. Here's the difference: A Stage I paragraph has just one opinion; the Stage II paragraph, on the other hand, has more than one opinion—the topic sentence, which is the main opinion, and several subtopic sentences, which are supporting opinions. Each subtopic sentence (covered in the next chapter) is a separate idea in the paragraph that helps support the main idea, the topic sentence. Let's look at an example (the subtopic sentences are italicized):

> My sister—nine years older than I am and now married—is one of the kindest people I have ever known. *During her spare time, Laurie often does something thoughtful for other people.* One year when I was hospitalized during my birthday, she spent a week making me a beautifully decorated card filled with her imagination and love. Countless times she has baked a batch of fudge-almond brownies for a new neighbor, for one of the elderly people nearby, or just for us. *Even when Laurie has something to do, she goes out of her way to be kind.* I remember when I was only eight years old and had been excited about the New Mexico State Fair for days. Mom had to work, so nobody could take me. But Laurie broke her date to go swimming with her boyfriend and, despite ninety-eight-degree heat and huge crowds, spent the afternoon with me. Although she must have regretted giving up her date, she was laughing and cheerful the whole time. Because of the kindness and love I felt from my sister Laurie, I look back on my childhood as a happy time.

Here's an outline of the paragraph:

Topic Sentence: Laurie is kind.
   Subtopic Sentence: She is kind when she has spare time.
      Specific Support: Birthday card.
      Specific Support: Baking brownies.
   Subtopic Sentence: She is kind when she is busy.
      Specific Support: Taking me to the fair.
Reworded Topic Sentence: Laurie is a kind person.

Notice that each subtopic sentence has the kind of specific support we discussed in Chapter 2. We use examples here, but statistics and statements by authorities would do as well.

Notice also that if you remove the subtopic sentences above, you would have a Stage I paragraph. Sometimes the relationship between Stage I and Stage II paragraphs is not so simple. You could add subtopic sentences to the Boundary Waters Canoe Area paragraph in Chapter 1, but you would end up with a worse paragraph because the support is so meager—the paragraph would have more topic and subtopic sentences than support sentences. Also, some Stage I paragraphs cannot become Stage II paragraphs because they were never divided into subtopic ideas. The sample paragraphs about fearing mathematics and learning to study faster in the exercises for Chapter 5, for example, do not have subtopic ideas, so you could not easily convert them into Stage II paragraphs.

Let's look now at a general model of the Stage II paragraph:

Topic Sentence
   Subtopic Sentence
      Specific Support
      Specific Support
   Subtopic Sentence
      Specific Support
      Specific Support
   Subtopic Sentence
      Specific Support
      Specific Support
Reworded Topic Sentence

This outline is not rigid, of course. Your Stage II paragraph may have two, three, or four subtopic sentences, and each subtopic sentence may have one to four items of support, depending on the subject and your approach to it. The paragraph above, for instance, had just two subtopic sentences, and one of those subtopic sentences has just one item of support—a narrative example.

Our sample paragraph above might have worked as a Stage I paragraph without subtopic sentences, but some paragraphs are so complex that they need subtopic sentences just to keep the reader (and maybe the writer) from getting lost. Look at this one:

Although apparently just an assortment of oddities from the National Museum of American History, a 1980 special exhibit called "The Nation's Attic" struck me as a tribute to American ingenuity. *One part of the exhibit demonstrated the ingenious ways Americans have found to shape everyday items.* For instance, a large collection of hand sewing accessories—hundreds of thimbles, needle cases, sewing cases, and pincushions—showed how simple things could be made more useful, more beautiful, or more entertaining. *More imaginative, though, were the things made apparently just because Americans wanted to accept the challenge of making them.* There was an intricate model of the U.S. Capitol constructed entirely of glass rods. Someone else had engraved the Lord's Prayer on a single grain of rice. And a group of chemical engineers had even managed to do the proverbial "undoable": they had actually created a silk purse from a sow's ear—just to prove it could be done. *The most interesting part of the exhibit to me, however, was some of the bizarre but ingenious failures among the models submitted for approval to the U.S. Patent Office.* I haven't been able to forget an early attempt at creating an electric razor. The inventor had mounted some razor blades on a rotating wheel so it looked something like the paddle wheel of a riverboat, and this wheel was attached to a small handheld electric motor. There were no guards to control the depth at which the blades cut, so anyone foolish enough to use the razor would no doubt have lost much more than a few whiskers from his face. Still, although I would never have sampled this inventor's work, I had to respect his resourcefulness. This invention, like the other unusual items in "The Nation's Attic," showed the mark of American ingenuity.

Here is an outline of the paragraph:

Topic Sentence: "The Nation's Attic" was a tribute to American ingenuity.

Subtopic Sentence: Some everyday items were ingenious.

Specific Support: Sewing items.

Subtopic Sentence: Some items made just for the challenge were imaginative.

Specific Support: Capitol from glass rods.

Specific Support: Lord's Prayer on grain of rice.

Specific Support: Silk purse from sow's ear.

      Subtopic Sentence: Some bizarre failures were ingenious.
      Specific Support: Attempt to create electric razor.
Reworded Topic Sentence: The unusual items showed American
                       ingenuity.

You might notice that the last sentence of the sample paragraph ties together the last item of support with all those that preceded it. That's not a necessary attribute of a reworded topic sentence, but it works nicely here.

Notice that even though a paragraph follows a model, as does the paragraph above, it can still be very good writing. The model is like a skeleton, and the content is like the body on that skeleton. We know that most people have skeletons that look about alike, but to a man looking at a woman—or to a woman looking at a man—the bodies can appear considerably different. Similarly, the content of an essay—what *you* have to say—can make an essay rather dowdy or very appealing.

EXERCISES

A. Outline this paragraph.

> To play water polo well, you have to learn to cheat. The only way you can keep the ball is by making a few slightly illegal moves. Pushing off your opponent's stomach can give you the elbowroom necessary to make a good pass or score a goal. Likewise, kneeing your attacker in the ribs can keep him from stealing the ball while you are setting up a play. When the opposing team does get possession, the unapproved solution for retrieving the ball is again through cheating. Pulling back on your adversary's leg is an effective means of slowing him down to give you a fairer chance at guarding him. But the most effective method of getting the ball is simply to pull his suit down, which immediately stops all his competitive activity. Fortunately, water polo is played in the water, since it hides the cheating all players must do in order to be successful.

Topic Sentence: _____

   Subtopic Sentence: _____

      Specific Support: _____

      Specific Support: _____

   Subtopic Sentence: _____

Specific Support: _____

Specific Support: _____

Reworded Topic Sentence: _____

B. Outline this paragraph.

My five-year old sister, Carol, is a tomboy. She is constantly in-volved in some type of rough activity. If she is playing football with her seven-year-old brother's friends, she always manages to hit one of the boys so hard that she incapacitates him for the rest of the game, usually sending him crying to his mother. Carol's friends are also evidence of her tomboyishness. When asked to tell the names of her school friends, she responds with Tom, Fred, Mark, John, and numerous other boys' names, but not with a single Mary, Barb, Kathy, or Joan. For her last birthday party, Carol invited seven boys and one girl. The one girl was her mother, as Mom had baked the cake and would be cleaning up afterward. So although Carol is physically a girl, her activities and friends show that at heart she is a tomboy.

Topic Sentence: _____

Subtopic Sentence: _____

Specific Support: _____

Subtopic Sentence: _____

Specific Support: _____

Specific Support: _____

Reworded Topic Sentence: _____

CHAPTER 7

Support: Subtopic Sentences

A subtopic sentence is very much like a topic sentence. Both state opinions that require specific support, and both are divisible into two parts: the subject, which must be limited; and the opinion, which must be precise. The difference is that a subtopic sentence serves as a *support idea* to help convince your readers to accept your main idea, the topic sentence. Theoretically, if you can persuade your readers to accept each subtopic sentence, then they should accept your topic sentence as well.

The precise opinion in each subtopic sentence is usually identical to the precise opinion in the topic sentence. The first sample paragraph in the last chapter, for example, used the subtopic sentences that "Laurie is *kind* during her spare time" and "Laurie is *kind* when she's busy" to convince us that "Laurie is *kind*."

In Part IV of this book, we'll examine in detail four good ways to develop and organize your support ideas for a paragraph or theme. Rather than distract you at this point with such a long discussion, we'll present in this chapter a quick but effective way to find support ideas by using subtopic sentences: subtopic sentences usually answer the questions "Why?," "How?," or "When?" about the topic sentence.

SUBTOPIC SENTENCE: "WHY?"

One of the easiest ways to find subtopic sentences for your paragraph is to state the topic sentence and then ask "Why?" If you wish to support the topic sentence "Highly competitive team sports can be psychologically damaging to young children," ask yourself, "*Why* can they be psychologically damaging?" You might decide that they can damage a child's view of himself and that they can damage a child's view of his peers. Next, you need specific support for each subtopic sentence. You believe that, if you can support these two subtopic sentences, you may well convince the reader that the sports can be psychologically damaging. Here is a possible outline:

> **Topic Sentence:** Highly competitive team sports can be psychologically damaging to young children.
>
> **Subtopic Sentence:** They can damage the child's view of himself.

Specific Support:	Bartholomew Wilkerson withdrew socially after missing a goal in soccer that cost his team the game.
Specific Support:	A recent survey by *Child Psychology* shows that 64% of the children in such sports suffer at least temporary emotional damage as a direct result.
Subtopic Sentence:	They can damage the child's view of his peers.
Specific Support:	A school counselor asserts that children like Bartholomew feel threatened by the other children in their school.
Specific Support:	This happened to Bartholomew, who avoided the playground during recess and the cafeteria during lunch.
Reworded Topic Sentence:	Therefore, highly competitive team sports can damage children psychologically.

In the paragraph above the subtopic sentences provide some reasons why the topic sentence is true, and the specific support provides the concrete evidence for those subtopic sentences.

Notice that a subtopic sentence answering the question "Why?" can always be joined to the topic sentence by the word *because:* "Highly competitive team sports can damage a child psychologically *because* they can damage the child's view of himself and *because* they can damage his view of his peers. Whenever you write a Stage II paragraph with "Why?" subtopic sentences, test them by joining them to the topic sentence with the word *because.*

SUBTOPIC SENTENCE: "HOW?"

Another common type of subtopic sentence answers the question "How?" Look at this paragraph that has subtopic sentences answering the question "How?":

Topic Sentence:	Heavy rush hour traffic brings out the worst in many drivers.
Subtopic Sentence:	Traffic conditions make some drivers overly nervous.
Specific Support:	Uncle Billy, usually a calm and careful driver, becomes so flustered in rush hour traffic that he can't carry on a conversation and forgets to check the

	rearview mirror when he changes lanes.
Specific Support:	A 1980 study of traffic flow in the Los Angeles area showed that the average waiting time at freeway entrance ramps increased to 1.5 minutes during rush hour because of the number of drivers who were afraid to merge into the heavy stream of cars.
Subtopic Sentence:	Heavy rush hour traffic reinforces the aggressiveness of some drivers.
Specific Support:	Often drivers follow too closely during rush hour because they're afraid other drivers might slip in ahead of them.
Specific Support:	Drivers continue into intersections on yellow lights even though they will get caught there and block cross traffic.
Specific Support:	A psychologist who has studied driver reactions concluded that "stress conditions of rush hour traffic cause physical and emotional reactions like those of a soldier in combat."
Reworded Topic Sentence:	Rush hour traffic conditions show many drivers at their worst.

Notice that these subtopic sentences clearly answer the question "How?" and not the question "Why?" "Why?" subtopic sentences probably would state something about the cause-effect relationship between rush hour traffic and the way drivers present themselves in it; "How?" subtopic sentences, on the other hand, show the results of the traffic on driver behavior.

We need to add a word of caution here. Sometimes subtopic sentences clearly answer "Why?" and sometimes they clearly answer "How?" At other times the questions appear to overlap. In other words, sometimes we can't be sure which of these two questions the subtopic sentences answer. Don't worry. The fine distinctions you would have to make are more fitting for a class in philosophy or semantics than for one in composition. Treat these questions for what they are—a quick and effective way to find subtopic sentences.

SUBTOPIC SENTENCE: "WHEN?"

Another type of subtopic sentence answers the question "When?" For example, to show that your roommate is constantly sleepy, you could ask yourself "When?" The resulting paragraph might look like this one.

Topic Sentence: My roommate is constantly sleepy.
Subtopic Sentence: He is sleepy in the morning when he gets up.
Specific Support: He fumbles with the alarm clock.
Specific Support: He once put his trousers on backward.
Subtopic Sentence: He is sleepy when he is in class.
Specific Support: He once fell asleep in Math III and crunched his jaw on the desk.
Specific Support: He does not even remember the subject of the lecture he attended yesterday in chemistry.
Subtopic Sentence: He is sleepy in the evening.
Specific Support: His typical study position is a comatose sprawl with his head on his desk.
Specific Support: He is always in bed by 8:30 P.M.
Reworded Topic Sentence: My roommate is sleepy all the time.

PARALLEL SUBTOPIC SENTENCES

In the examples in this chapter, all the subtopic sentences within a one-paragraph essay answer the same question, "Why?," "How?," or "When?" Your Stage II paragraphs should do the same. In other words, if you are supporting the idea "Hitchhiking is dangerous" in a Stage II paragraph, do not answer the question "Why?" for one subtopic sentence ("Hitchhiking is dangerous because too many drivers are deranged") and the question "When?" for another subtopic sentence ("Hitchhiking is dangerous at night, when the streets are poorly lighted"). These ideas may both work to support your topic sentence, but they do not work well together. They are not parallel and seem like a mixture of apples and oranges when you are selling only apples. Once you have outlined your Stage II paragraph, be sure your subtopic sentences answer the same questions: "Why?," "How?," or "When?"

EXERCISES

A. For each of the subtopic sentences below, invent (in other words, make up) subtopic sentences and specific support. Be sure all your subtopic sentences within the paragraph answer the same question: "Why?," "How?," or "When?"

1. TV video games are a waste of time.

Subtopic Sentence: _____

_____

Specific Support: _____

_____

_____

_____

_____

Specific Support: _____

_____

_____

_____

_____

Subtopic Sentence: _____

_____

Specific Support: _____

_____

_____

_____

_____

Specific Support: _____

_____

_____

_____

_____

2. Railroads are an excellent way to transport perishable agricultural products over long distances.

Subtopic Sentence: _____

_____

Specific Support: _____

_____

_____

_____

_____

Specific Support: _____

_____

_____

_____

_____

Subtopic Sentence: _____

_____

    Specific Support: _____

_____

_____

_____

    Specific Support: _____

_____

_____

_____

_____

3.   Flying is dangerous.

    Subtopic Sentence: _____

_____

    Specific Support: _____

_____

_____

_____

    Specific Support: _____

_____

_____

_____

_____

Subtopic Sentence: _____

_____

Specific Support: _____

_____

_____

_____

_____

Specific Support: _____

_____

_____

_____

_____

B. If your instructor requests, outline the opposite of all the above topic sentences. In other words, convince us that "TV video games are worthwhile," and so on.

C. In the exercises above you outlined Stage II paragraphs. Select the one that interests you the most and use the evidence you invented to write the paragraph.

D. Write a Stage II paragraph convincing us that somebody you know has a positive (pleasant, good) or a negative (unpleasant, bad) characteristic. For an example see the paragraph about Laurie, the first sample paragraph in Chapter 6.

E. Write a Stage II paragraph explaining how something you have observed impressed you. The sample paragraph in Chapter 6 about "The Nation's Attic" could have been a response to this exercise.

CHECKLIST FOR THE ONE-PARAGRAPH ESSAY

TOPIC SENTENCE

_____ Does the topic sentence state an opinion to be supported?

_____ Is the topic sentence the first sentence in the paragraph?

_____ Is the subject of the topic sentence limited?

_____ Is the opinion precise?

SUPPORT

_____ Does the support begin with the second sentence of the paragraph?

_____ Is the support specific enough to be convincing?

_____ Do the items of support clearly belong with the topic sentence (unity)?

_____ Do you explain your support fully so that the relation to the topic sentence is clear (coherence)?

_____ Does each item of support include a reminder of the opinion in the topic sentence (coherence)?

_____ Do you have transitions at the critical locations (coherence)?

CONCLUSION

_____ Does the last sentence of the paragraph reword the topic sentence?

OTHER

_____ Is the paragraph convincing?

_____ Is the paragraph interesting?

_____ Are the words precise and colorful?

_____ Are grammar and sentence structure correct?

_____ Are all the words spelled correctly?

_____ Is the paper neat?

PART III

THE FIVE-PARAGRAPH ESSAY

A five-paragraph essay is a handy device for learning to write longer papers. The first and last paragraphs are the introduction and conclusion, two new types of paragraph most longer papers need. The three central paragraphs provide enough material to justify a full-length introduction and conclusion but still keep the paper short enough to be manageable—both for you and for your instructor.

You'll also begin writing about more serious topics in this part. So far you've depended entirely on your own experiences for support; you'll still present your experiences here, but you'll supplement them with occasional support from books and magazines. Of course, we don't expect you to learn the fundamentals of the multiparagraph essay and the fundamentals of documentation at the same time, so we present in this section a simplified system of documentation you can use until you study the research paper in Part V.

CHAPTER 8

Overview of the Five-Paragraph Essay

You may have noticed that your paragraphs are turning into monsters. They are so long that they seem more like small themes than one-paragraph essays. You are right. Often you have so much to say about a topic that you end up writing more than you had intended. At that point you are better off dividing your large single paragraph into several units with an introduction and a conclusion. Your multiparagraph essay will resemble the Stage II paragraph except that the Stage II topic sentence becomes a full-length introduction, the Stage II subtopic sentences and their specific support become complete central paragraphs, and the Stage II reworded topic sentence becomes a full-length conclusion:

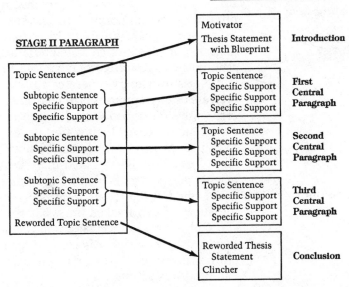

FIVE-PARAGRAPH ESSAY

The introduction begins with a *motivator*, which gains the reader's attention; follows with the *thesis statement*, which presents the main idea of the essay; and includes a *blueprint,* which summarizes the topic sentences that will begin each of the central paragraphs.

Each central paragraph supports an opinion that in turn helps support the thesis statement. The central paragraphs are basically like the one-paragraph essays you have been writing (either State I or Stage II) except that the reworded topic sentences are no longer necessary.

The conclusion begins with a *reworded thesis statement,* which reminds the reader of the theme's main point, and finishes with a *clincher,* a sentence or two that give the essay a sense of finality.

Here is a sample five-paragraph essay:

Motivator

Do you realize that newly born children are not even aware that parts of their bodies belong to them? I learned this fascinating fact in my psychology course from a book that says a baby "lies on his back, kicking his heels and watching the little fists flying past his face. But only very slowly does he come to know that they are attached to him and he can control them" (Mary Ann Spencer Pulaski, *Understanding Piaget,* p. 21). Children certainly have a lot of learning and adjusting to do before they can see the world—and themselves—through grown-up eyes. And as children pass through this remarkable process of growing up, they often do some humorous things, especially in learning to speak, in discovering that all objects do not have human characteristics, and in attempting to imitate others around them.

Thesis Statement

Blueprint

Topic Sentence

Specific Support

Not surprisingly, one area in which children are often humorous is in learning to speak. I remember one time I was talking to a friend on the phone while my little sister, Betsy, seemed to be playing inattentively on the floor nearby. After I hung up, Betsy asked me, "Why is the teacher going to give Janet an old tomato!" At first I couldn't figure out what Betsy was talking about. When I asked her what she meant, she said, "You said if Janet doesn't hand in her homework, the teacher is going to give her an old tomato." Finally I caught on. The word I had used was *ultimatum.*

Topic Sentence

Specific Support

Specific Support

Specific Support

Topic Sentence

Specific Support

Specific Support

Reworded Thesis

Clincher

Children can also be funny in the way they "humanize" the objects around them. According to my psychology book, "Up to four or five years old, the child believes anything may be endowed with purpose and conscious activity. A ball may refuse to be thrown straight, or a 'naughty' chair may be responsible for bumping him" (Pulaski, p. 45). I, myself, can still remember one vivid and scary afternoon when I was sure the sun was following me around just waiting for the right moment to get me. I can also remember a time, this one not scary, when Betsy stood at the top of the stairs and yelled to her shoes at the bottom, "Shoes! Get up here!"

Another way in which children are sometimes funny is in their attempts to imitate what they see around them. All children look pretty silly when they dress up like their mothers and fathers and play "house." My psychology book tells of a more interesting example, though. The famous psychologist Piaget wrote of the time his sixteen-month-old daughter quietly watched a visiting little boy throw a tantrum in trying to get out of his play-pen. Piaget's daughter later thought it would be fun to try the same thing: "The next day, she herself screamed in her play-pen and tried to move it, stamping her foot lightly several times in succession. The imitation of the whole scene was most striking" (quoted in Pulaski, p. 81). This may be the kind of humor, however, that loses its savor quickly, especially if you are part of the family.

Little children are funny creatures to watch, aren't they? But as we laugh, we have to admire, too, because the humorous mistakes are but temporary side trips that children take on the amazingly complicated journey to maturity, a long way from the beginning where they lie in wonder in their cribs, silently watching the strange, fingered spacecraft passing, back and forth, before their infant eyes.

Now look at an outline of the essay:

INTRODUCTION

Motivator: Children have many things to learn and adjust to as they grow up— including the awareness of the parts of their bodies.
Thesis: Children often do humorous things.
Blueprint: They're often humorous in learning to speak, in discovering that all objects do not have human characteristics, and in attempting to imitate others.

FIRST CENTRAL PARAGRAPH

Topic Sentence: Children are often humorous in learning to speak.
Specific Support: Betsy mistook *old tomato* for *ultimatum.*

SECOND CENTRAL PARAGRAPH

Topic Sentence: Children "humanize" the objects around them.
Specific Support: Book says children blame balls and chairs as though the things were conscious.
Specific Support: I thought the sun was out to get me.
Specific Support: Betsy ordered her shoes to climb the stairs.

THIRD CENTRAL PARAGRAPH

Topic Sentence: Children attempt to imitate what they see.
Specific Support: They dress like their parents.
Specific Support: Piaget's daughter imitated a tantrum a visiting child threw.

CONCLUSION

Reworded Thesis: Children are funny creatures to watch.
Clincher: Reminder of the motivator that children have a lot of learning and adjusting to do.

The sample theme is a mixture of support from the writer's personal experiences with children—especially her sister Betsy—and her recent knowledge from a psychology book. You might notice that the thesis—that children are funny—did not come from the book; only the support did. The writer used the book not so much for ideas as for supporting facts. Otherwise, the five-paragraph essay might have turned into just a book report.

Until now, you've been writing most of your papers based on your personal experiences. Though you can stretch that kind of paper into a five-paragraph essay (as in the exercise for this chapter), you can probably write more serious and substantial papers by referring occasionally to outside sources. We'd be foolish, though, to insist that you learn the fundamentals of the five-paragraph essay and the fundamentals of documentation at the same time. That is generally too much for anyone to handle in one step, so we cover documentation in Part V, "The Research Paper." But to permit you to use some outside sources now, we've designed what we call a "makeshift" system of documentation. You should realize that this system is just a temporary tool so that you can write good multiparagraph essays without struggling with all the details of documentation.

Here's our makeshift system:

1. Put quotation marks around all words you take directly from a source.

2. At the end of every sentence in which you use somebody else's *words or ideas*, identify the source in parentheses:

a. For a book, give the author's full name, the title of the book (underlined), and the page number of the material you use. If you use the same book more than once in your paper, give just the author and page number for the second and additional references.

b. For a magazine article, give the author's full name (if known), the title of the article (in quotation marks), the title of the magazine (underlined), the date, and the page number. Again, if you refer to the same article more than once, after the first reference give just either the author or the title of the magazine followed by the page number.

c. For something else—an interview, perhaps, or a classroom discussion—improvise. Give whatever information you can, but always give something. Don't leave words or ideas undocumented just because you haven't yet learned the proper format.

Proper documentation serves two purposes: it tells your readers whenever you are using borrowed material, and it gives enough information for them to be able to find your source. Our makeshift system serves only the first purpose, because it may not always be complete enough for your reader to find your book or magazine. As a result, your instructor may ask you to keep your sources handy so they can be checked.

EXERCISE

Outline this five-paragraph essay:

When a person thinks of that old-time, small-town doctor, he usually envisions a mannerly, dignified gentleman. However, this image did not fit my Uncle Rodney, a doctor in the small town of Bandon, Wyoming. Instead, Doctor Rodney was an obnoxious person because he had an annoying habit of speaking in crude, incoherent sentences; he had sloppy eating habits; and he was a messy smoker.

Probably Doctor Rodney's most irritating trait was his crude way of speaking. For example, I recall a particularly embarrassing moment during a family reunion at my mother-in-law's house when Dr. Rodney was asked to say a blessing before dinner. He managed a "Hump, bump, grump," or so it sounded, and almost immediately added "Goddammit" as he knocked over a bowl of grated corn he was grabbing. As a result, my mother-in-law—a very religious person—was mortified. On another occasion, Dr. Rodney's nurse said, "It's a good thing I can interpret what Dr. Rodney says and smooth over the rough feelings, or we would be out of patients."

Additionally, Doctor Rodney bothered many people with his messy eating habits. He shoveled food into his mouth at such an alarming rate that often he could not catch his breath. My brother-in-law once remarked, "When I see Uncle Rodney eat, I think of jackals devouring their kill." Furthermore, Doctor Rodney always finished his meal long before anyone else; then he would make a nauseating slurping sound by sucking air and saliva through the gaps between his top front teeth while he waited for everybody else to finish. Because of his atrocious eating habits, none of Doctor Rodney's neighbors invited him to dinner.

Doctor Rodney was also disliked because he was an inconsiderate smoker. Everywhere he went, he left a trail of ashes, a terrible stench, and wet, chewed-up cigar butts. After his death, the office cleaning lady confided that the townspeople used to bet on how many days would pass before anyone saw Dr. Rodney without a spot of tobacco juice on his shirt. Naturally, all the local children learned not to be downwind from him because no one could easily tolerate his odor of stale tobacco.

Clearly, Dr. Rodney was an obnoxious person whose talking, eating, and smoking habits alienated him from even his own family. He was indeed lucky that the town had only one doctor, or he might not have been employed.

INTRODUCTION

Motivator:
Thesis:
Blueprint:

FIRST CENTRAL PARAGRAPH

Topic Sentence:
    Specific Support:
    Specific Support:

SECOND CENTRAL PARAGRAPH

Topic Sentence:
    Specific Support:
    Specific Support:
    Specific Support;
    Specific Support:

THIRD CENTRAL PARAGRAPH

Topic Sentence:
    Specific Support:
    Specific Support:
    Specific Support:

CONCLUSION

Reworded Thesis:
Clincher:

CHAPTER 9

Thesis Statement with Blueprint

The thesis statement of the five-paragraph essay, or theme, is the single-sentence statement that you intend the entire essay to support. The thesis statement has a limited subject with a precise opinion about that subject; and in its basic form, the thesis statement says that *"limited subject is precise opinion."*

Does all this sound familiar? Do we seem to be talking about the topic sentence of the one-paragraph essay? In a way we are. Like the topic sentence, the thesis statement of the multiparagraph essay is the thought at the head of the body; it is the opinion that you will persuade your reader to accept.

RELATIONSHIP OF THESIS STATEMENT TO TOPIC SENTENCE

Stated simply, the thesis statement is to the multiparagraph essay as the topic sentence is to the one-paragraph essay. The thesis statement does not necessarily state a more general (or "larger") opinion than a topic sentence does. Instead, the thesis statement is an opinion that has more support: it is supported by several paragraphs rather than by only one.

Still, since a thesis statement is like a topic sentence, what is true for the topic sentence is also true for the thesis statement. Therefore, to form your thesis statement, you need only approach your material as you would to form a topic sentence: you must limit the subject and then form a precise opinion about that subject. No matter how you word the thesis statement, you may always reduce it to the basic sentence form of *"limited subject is precise opinion."*

BLUEPRINT

If you are a careful reader of chapter titles, you noticed that this chapter is called not "Thesis Statement" but "Thesis Statement with Blueprint." What is a blueprint for a theme, and why do you want one? As the name

66

suggests, the blueprint is like an architect's pattern for the structure that he plans to build—only you are the architect and the structure you intend to build is your essay. The rest of the chapter tells you what the theme's blueprint is and how to combine it with the thesis statement, resulting in "thesis statement with blueprint."

In the preceding chapter, the overview of the five-paragraph essay, you learned that the blueprint "summarizes the topic sentences that will begin each of the central paragraphs" of the essay. Thus, your blueprint tells the readers briefly how you plan to develop your argument. Combining thesis statement and blueprint, you tell your readers both *what* you intend to persuade them to believe (thesis statement) and *how* you will go about persuading them (blueprint).

Let's examine a blueprint with its thesis statement. The topic sentence for a Stage II paragraph—"Highly competitive team sports can be psychologically damaging to young children"—could be supported by three subtopic or support ideas: "They can damage a child's view of himself," "They can damage a child's view of his peers," and "They can damage a child's view of adults." If we expand the support for the topic sentence, the length of the argument will require a five-paragraph essay. In this case, each of the "support ideas" will become a topic sentence of a central paragraph, and the topic sentence of the Stage II paragraph will become the thesis statement of the five-paragraph essay, as follows:

STAGE II PARAGRAPH		FIVE-PARAGRAPH ESSAY
Topic Sentence	Highly competitive team sports can be psychologically damaging to young children.	Thesis Statement
Subtopic Sentence	They can damage a child's view of himself.	First Central Paragraph Topic Sentence
Subtopic Sentence	They can damage a child's view of his peers.	Second Central Paragraph Topic Sentence
Subtopic Sentence	They can damage a child's view of adults.	Third Central Paragraph Topic Sentence

Now, to form a blueprint we combine the basic ideas from the central paragraphs in the order they appear:

> Because they can damage a child's view of himself, his peers, and adults. . . .

Combining this blueprint with the thesis, we produce a thesis statement with blueprint:

> Because they can damage a child's view of himself, his peers, and adults, highly competitive team sports can be psychologically damaging to young children.

But why use a blueprint? Quite frankly, the blueprint is a mechanical aid to your reader and to you. And equally frankly, the blueprint is not always necessary. Still, it is an excellent aid at this stage of your writing, helping you understand the basic organization of the five-paragraph essay. You should use it in your first few long papers.

MECHANICS OF THE BLUEPRINT

Since the blueprint is a summary of the ideas of the central paragraphs of the multiparagraph essay, the mechanics of the blueprint come from the relationship of support ideas to the thesis statement. You've learned that each subtopic sentence of a Stage II paragraph answers a "Why?," "How?," or "When?" question about the topic sentence. Central paragraph topic sentences have the same relationship to their thesis statement. Thus, since the blueprint outlines the ideas of the central paragraphs, each item of the blueprint will answer a "Why?," "How?," or "When?" question.

"Why?" Blueprint   If we ask "Why?" about the thesis statement, the answer will be "because." Therefore, the "Why?" blueprint can always begin with *because*. Why can highly competitive team sports be psychologically damaging to young children?

> *Because* they can damage a child's view of himself, his peers, and adults, . . .

"How?" Blueprint   Phrases beginning with *by, with,* and *through* may answer "How?" questions. In addition, since "How?" questions are sometimes similar to "Why?" questions, *because* may also begin the "How?" blueprint. For example, how does Wanda distract you?

With her singing, her eating, and her talking, . . .

OR

Because of her singing, her eating, and her talking, . . .

OR

By singing, eating, and talking as I try to study, . . .

OR

Through her singing, her eating, and her talking, . . .

"When?" Blueprint   Finally, if we somehow stretch the Stage II idea of the sleepy roommate into a five-paragraph essay, we would ask "When?" about the thesis "My roommate is constantly sleepy." "When?" would be answered by "when," as follows:

When he gets up in the morning, sits in class, or studies in the evening, . . .

THESIS WITH BLUEPRINT

You will sometimes see multiparagraph essays without blueprints, although the introduction will usually at least imply how the thesis will be developed (the sample theme in Chapter 15 works this way). And you may also see themes in which the blueprint appears in a sentence or sentences separate from the thesis; the blueprint sentences still accompany the thesis, but appear in the introduction before or after the thesis idea. Nevertheless, you can easily attach the blueprint to the thesis sentence, and this single-sentence combination makes clear the relationship of development pattern and main idea. Such a combination of thesis statement and blueprint may take one of two forms:

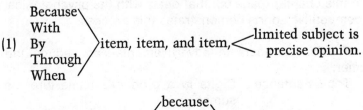

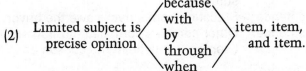

Thus, sample blueprints you just saw could combine with thesis statements as follows:

(Why?)   Because they can damage a child's view of himself, his peers, and adults, highly competitive team sports can be psychologically damaging to young children.

OR

Highly competitive team sports can be psychologically damaging to young children because they can damage a child's view of himself, his peers, and adults.

(How?)   By singing, eating, and talking as I try to study, Wanda distracts me.

OR

Wanda distracts me by singing, eating, and talking as I try to study.

(When?)   When he gets up in the morning, sits in class, or studies in the evening, my roommate is constantly sleepy.

OR

My roommate is constantly sleepy—when he gets up in the morning, sits in class, or studies in the evening.

No matter which form you choose, the combination of thesis statement and blueprint will tell your readers what you want them to believe and how you are going to persuade them.

EXERCISES

A. Each of the problems in this exercise provides a thesis statement and three topic sentences for the body paragraphs of a five-paragraph essay. You must combine necessary ideas from the topic sentences with the thesis statement to form a "thesis statement with blueprint." The example in this chapter (page 68) that deals with the psychological damage of competitive sports demonstrates this process.

    1.   Thesis: Numbers in advertisements can seduce the consumer.

      Topic Sentence: Digits in a product's name lure the consumer.

      Topic Sentence: Statistics from surveys awe the buyer.

      Topic Sentence: Other numbers sprinkled through an advertisement overwhelm the consumer.

      Thesis with Blueprint: _____

_____

_____

2. Thesis: Pruning large shade trees requires expertise.
   Topic Sentence: Choosing which limbs to cut demands judgment.
   Topic Sentence: Sawing large lower limbs without damaging the trunk takes skill.
   Topic Sentence: Reaching small upper branches requires special techniques.

   Thesis with Blueprint: _____

   _____

   _____

3. Thesis: Restoring old houses is rewarding.
   Topic Sentence: Discovering the original interior below layers of changes is exciting.
   Topic Sentence: Working with one's hands is relaxing.
   Topic Sentence: Viewing the completed project is satisfying.

   Thesis with Blueprint: _____

   _____

   _____

4. Thesis: The linebacker position is demanding.
   Topic Sentence: Diagnosing the play requires intelligence.
   Topic Sentence: The number of directions in which the linebacker must be able to move requires agility.
   Topic Sentence: Still, the linebacker must have enough strength to stop the ball carrier.

   Thesis with Blueprint: _____

   _____

   _____

5. Thesis: Technical support systems provide today's meteorologists with better data for their predictions.
   Topic Sentence: Computerized historical records give a more detailed picture of seasonal weather patterns.
   Topic Sentence: Satellite photography provides better tracking of wind and cloud movements.

Topic Sentence: Modern communications networks allow more immediate access to weather data from widespread areas.

Thesis with Blueprint: _____

_____

_____

B.   Each problem below provides a thesis statement for a five-paragraph essay. Invent the three topic sentences to support each thesis, and then rewrite the thesis statement with a blueprint attached to it.

1.   Thesis: When the pack is not on the back, backpacking is exhilarating.

Topic Sentence: _____

Topic Sentence: _____

Topic Sentence: _____

Thesis with Blueprint: _____

_____

_____

2.   Thesis: My great-grandfather is finally beginning to show his age.

Topic Sentence: _____

Topic Sentence: _____

Topic Sentence: _____

Thesis with Blueprint: _____

_____

_____

3.   Thesis: Finding a part-time job is frustrating.

Topic Sentence: _____

Topic Sentence: _____

Topic Sentence: _____

Thesis with Blueprint: _____

_____

_____

CHAPTER 10

Central Paragraphs

Because your purpose in a theme is always to persuade the reader to accept your thesis, you need space to argue your point. Generally, the more fully you develop the evidence that supports your thesis, the more persuasive you'll be. Central paragraphs, which form the body of your theme, provide the needed space.

Each central paragraph, which is like a Stage I or Stage II paragraph, develops an opinion that in turn helps develop the thesis statement. Specific evidence in a central paragraph supports the paragraph's topic sentence, and the topic sentences, taken together, support the thesis. Therefore, if each central paragraph supports its own topic sentence, and if the topic sentences are properly related to each other and to the thesis, then the central paragraphs should persuade the reader to accept that thesis statement.

Three of the paragraphs of a five-paragraph essay are central paragraphs. Similarly, all but two paragraphs of any multiparagraph essay are central or body paragraphs. The two exceptions, introduction and conclusion, are discussed in Chapters 11 and 12; until you study these chapters, the Thesis Statement with Blueprint will suffice for both theme introduction and conclusion. For the moment, then, consider the form of the five-paragraph essay to be the following:

Thesis Statement with Blueprint

> First Central Paragraph

> Second Central Paragraph

> Third Central Paragraph

Thesis Statement with Blueprint

A body paragraph is very similar to a one-paragraph essay; that is, each one presents a topic sentence followed by specific support. You already know, for the most part, how to write this type of paragraph. This chapter deals with two differences: *omission of the reworded topic sentence* and *additions to the topic sentence.*

OMISSION OF THE REWORDED TOPIC SENTENCE

Every Stage I and Stage II paragraph essay, a unit complete in itself, has three basic parts: topic sentence, specific support, and reworded topic sentence. The reworded topic sentence provides a mark of finality to the argument. Think how frustrated you would feel if someone told you most of a story but failed to complete it. In the same way, arguments are more satisfying, and therefore more convincing, if the reader feels a sense of completion at the end of the essay.

A central paragraph, however, does not require this same mark of finality. Remember that a central paragraph does not present the entire argument of the theme. Instead, the development of the thesis is complete only after all central paragraphs are presented. Therefore, the mark of completion is one of the special functions of the concluding paragraph. Each central paragraph, then, ends without a reworded topic sentence; when the last item of specific support of a central paragraph is finished, so is that paragraph.

ADDITIONS TO THE TOPIC SENTENCE

Like a topic sentence for a one-paragraph essay, the topic sentence for a central paragraph presents the *main idea of the paragraph* in the basic form of "limited subject is precise opinion." However, the central-paragraph topic sentence has two additions—a *transition* from the preceding paragraph and a *reminder of the thesis.*

The first addition, the transition, provides theme coherence. Just as sentences within any paragraph must move smoothly from one to another, paragraphs within a theme must also flow together. The pieces of the total argument will not seem to combine unless the paragraphs that contain the pieces of argument also combine.

The second addition to the topic sentence, the reminder of the thesis, helps fit the central paragraph's main idea to the theme's main idea. The total argument will come together more easily if each central paragraph's idea (its topic sentence) connects to the theme's idea (the thesis statement). This addition, then, helps provide both coherence and unity for the theme.

Thus, a central-paragraph topic sentence includes these parts: a *transition,* a *reminder of the thesis,* and the *main idea of the paragraph.*

Let's examine central paragraph topic sentences in a five-paragraph essay. Remember the theme in Chapter 8 about the humorous things that children do? The thesis statement is "they [children] often do some humorous things." The topic sentence for the first central paragraph is as follows:

> Not surprisingly, one area in which children are often humorous is in learning to speak.

The parts of the topic sentence are these:

> Transition: The word "one," an explicit indication that the first of several items will be presented, helps alert the reader that the introduction is over and the support is beginning.
>
> Reminder of thesis: "humorous" repeats the key word from the thesis statement.
>
> Main idea of paragraph: The paragraph will focus on "learning to speak" as one way in which children can be humorous.

The topic sentence of the second paragraph is this:

> Children can also be funny in the way they "humanize" the objects around them.

The topic sentence parts are the following:

> Transition: "also" suggests that this is another (or second) indication of the truth of the thesis.
>
> Reminder of thesis: "funny" connects to "humorous" in the thesis.
>
> Main idea of paragraph: Children "humanize" the objects around them.

Finally, the third topic sentence is this:

> Another way in which children are funny is in their attempts to imitate what they see around them.

Topic sentence parts are these:

> Transition: "Another way" indicates movement to a third support idea.
>
> Reminder of thesis: Again, the word "funny" connects to the word "humorous" in the thesis.

Main idea of paragraph: This paragraph will be about the children's attempts to imitate what they see around them.

Because you must have space to develop your argument, you break it into parts—the arguments of the central paragraphs. Yet, like a jigsaw puzzle, a theme will never seem complete unless you connect the pieces. The additions to the topic sentence of each central paragraph help you to fit the central-paragraph main ideas to each other and to the thesis statement, creating a whole, the body of your theme.

EXERCISES

A. Each of the problems in this exercise provides a thesis statement and three topic sentences for the central paragraphs of a five-paragraph essay. Identify the transition, the reminder of thesis, and the main idea of the paragraph ("limited subject is precise opinion") for each topic sentence.

   1. Thesis: Pruning large shade trees requires expertise.
      First Topic Sentence: First, choosing which limbs to cut demands judgment.

         Transition: _____

         Reminder of thesis: _____

         Main idea of paragraph: _____

         _____

      Second Topic Sentence: Second, sawing lower limbs without damaging the trunk takes skill.

         Transition: _____

         Reminder of thesis: _____

         Main idea of paragraph: _____

         _____

      Third Topic Sentence: Finally, reaching small upper branches requires special techniques.

         Transition: _____

         Reminder of thesis: _____

         Main idea of paragraph: _____

         _____

   2. Thesis: Football's linebacker position requires a versatile athlete.

First Topic Sentence: As a play begins, the linebacker must use his intelligence to diagnose the offensive team's plan.

Transition: _____

Reminder of thesis: _____

Main idea of paragraph: _____

_____

Second Topic Sentence: As the play develops, the linebacker must be agile enough to move in any direction.

Transition: _____

Reminder of thesis: _____

Main idea of paragraph: _____

_____

Third Topic Sentence: Still, if the linebacker, bright and agile as he may be, hopes to end the play, he must be strong enough to stop the ball carrier.

Transition: _____

Reminder of thesis: _____

Main idea of paragraph: _____

_____

3. Thesis: Technical support systems provide today's meteorologists with better data for their predictions.
First Topic Sentence: For one thing, computerized historical records give a more detailed picture of seasonal weather patterns.

Transition: _____

Reminder of thesis: _____

Main idea of paragraph: _____

_____

Second Topic Sentence: Also, satellite photography provides better tracking of wind and cloud movements.

Transition: _____

Reminder of thesis: _____

Main idea of paragraph: _____

_____

Third Topic Sentence: Furthermore, modern communications networks allow more immediate access to weather data from widespread areas.

Transition: _____

Reminder of thesis: _____

Main idea of paragraph: _____

_____

B.   Each problem in this exercise provides a thesis statement and three main ideas for topic sentences for the central paragraphs of a five-paragraph essay. Use the main ideas to compose central-paragraph topic sentences; remember to include the three basic parts—transition, reminder of thesis, and main idea. Then identify the transition and reminder of thesis you used for each topic sentence.

1.   Thesis: Numbers in advertisements can seduce the consumer.
      Main idea: Digits in a product's name lure the consumer.
      Main idea: Statistics from surveys awe the buyer.
      Main idea: Other numbers sprinkled through an advertisement overwhelm the consumer.
      First Topic Sentence: _____

_____

Transition: _____

Reminder of thesis: _____

Second Topic Sentence: _____

_____

Transition: _____

Reminder of thesis: _____

Third Topic Sentence: _____

_____

Transition: _____

Reminder of thesis: _____

2.   Thesis: Restoring old houses is rewarding.
      Main idea: Discovering the original interior is exciting.
      Main idea: Working with one's hands is relaxing.
      Main idea: Viewing the completed project is satisfying.
      First Topic Sentence: _____

_____

Transition: _____

Reminder of thesis: _____

Second Topic Sentence: _____

_____

Transition: _____

Reminder of thesis: _____

Third Topic Sentence: _____

_____

Transition: _____

Reminder of thesis: _____

C. Recall for a minute the sample theme in Chapter 8 on the humorous things children do. In a way, the writer of that theme was an "expert" on children's funny behavior: she had been a child herself, and she had observed her sister (and undoubtedly many other children) growing up. She did not depend in that theme on any expertise in psychology, only on the behavior of children she had observed. The expertise she did use —from the book on Piaget—was highly interesting, of course, but it was not an essential part of the thesis statement, nor was it essential as support. You, too, are probably an "expert" in something. Perhaps you play golf well or understand how to tune an automobile engine or know every record the Beatles (remember them?) recorded. Choose something you know well and say something *significant* about it. Once you have something significant to say about your topic, turn that statement into a thesis statement with blueprint. Then, letting the thesis statement with blueprint serve as both the introduction and the conclusion, write the three central paragraphs of the five-paragraph essay (you'll write the full-length introduction and conclusion later as exercises for Chapters 11 and 12).

Be sure to use the same kind of detailed support for each central paragraph that you would use for a one-paragraph essay, and be sure that each of your topic sentences contains a transition from the previous paragraph, a reminder of the thesis statement, and the main idea of the paragraph.

If you use outside sources, use them only to find support, not to find a thesis. Otherwise, you'll find yourself merely paraphrasing someone else. Also, be sure to place quotation marks around all words you borrow directly. At the end of every sentence containing borrowed words or ideas, acknowledge your source in parentheses (look again at Chapter 8 if you've forgotten the rules for the makeshift documentation system).

CHAPTER 11

Introduction

The introduction to a theme serves two important purposes: it gains your readers' attention, and it tells your readers the main idea of the theme and how you will develop that idea. The part that gains their attention is the *motivator;* the part that tells them the main idea of the theme and its development is the *thesis statement with blueprint* (covered in Chapter 9). This chapter, though it has examples of thesis statements with blueprints, concentrates on motivators.

As you practice writing and look carefully at the writing of others, you will discover many effective ways of motivating your reader. Three of the simplest motivators are the *contrary opinion,* the *striking incident,* and the *striking statement.*

INTRODUCTION

> **Motivator:** contrary opinion, striking incident, or striking statement
> **Thesis Statement with Blueprint**

CONTRARY OPINION

The easiest way to begin a theme is to state the opinion your paper opposes, then make a transition to your thesis statement with blueprint. Basically, you state what the poor, misguided fools believe, then state your opinion—the one your theme is going to prove:

INTRODUCTION

> **What the Opposition Says** (the statement opposite to your thesis)
> **Transition**
> **What You Say** (your thesis statement with blueprint)

The transition is particularly important in this kind of introduction because you must move clearly and smoothly from the position you oppose to the position you support.

Here is a sample introduction to an essay showing that smoking is a disgusting habit:

Motivator

Transition
Thesis Statement
with Blueprint

> Some people think that smoking makes them appear sophisticated and mysterious, perhaps even seductive. They become Humphrey Bogart in *Casablanca* or Lauren Bacall in *To Have and Have Not*. Those people, however, are wrong. Smoking is really a disgusting habit —messy, irritating to others, and possibly harmful to the nonsmoker.

Notice that the thesis statement and blueprint are obvious, not tucked away shyly. In this introduction the reader knows that he has read the main idea of the theme and how it will be developed.

Here is another sample introduction using the contrary opinion as a motivator:

Motivator

Transition
Thesis Statement
with Blueprint

> Just two days ago Esther Hermann remarked that the interns she knows are so good that she would rather be treated by one of them than by a resident physician. Esther never was very smart. Unfortunately, today's interns are usually incompetent—overworked, poorly trained, and inadequately supervised.

For an additional example of the contrary opinion as a motivator, look at the five-paragraph essay in the exercise for Chapter 8.

STRIKING INCIDENT

One of the flashiest ways to begin a theme is to tell the reader a brief story (sometimes called an anecdote) that is somehow related to your thesis statement. You will lure the reader into your paper because he is curious about the story. By the time he has finished the story, only two or three sentences later, sheer momentum will carry him into your thesis statement with blueprint.

Here is a sample introduction that begins with a striking incident:

Motivator

Thesis Statement with Blueprint

I walked into the living room, turned on the television, and settled back comfortably into my recliner. When the picture finally came on the screen, I was confronted by a sensuous blonde slinking toward me, her eyes looking straight into mine. She whispered provocatively, "I like a Marlboro man." I was ready to start smoking. I never did, though, because, blondes and Marlboro men notwithstanding, smoking is a disgusting habit—messy, irritating to others, and possibly harmful to the nonsmoker.

Notice that this introduction contains a transition ("I never did, though . . .") between the motivator and thesis statement with blueprint. Some introductions need such a transition—like the one above and all those that begin with the contrary opinion—while others move smoothly from the motivator to the thesis statement with blueprint without any transition words:

Motivator

Thesis Statement with Blueprint

On June 11, 1977, Esther Hermann stumbled into the emergency room of the Coronado General Hospital, complaining of double vision and a headache. The intern on duty diagnosed exhaustion and prescribed three days of bed rest. Two days later, Esther was dead, killed by one of the many incompetent interns who have been loosed on the American public—overworked, undertrained, and poorly supervised.

Transitions, then, are not always necessary if the striking incident leads directly to the thesis statement.

STRIKING STATEMENT

Another easy way to gain your reader's interest is to begin the essay as though you are angry or disturbed about something. After all, if we are walking along and hear someone yelling, we will probably stop because we are curious. Here is a sample introduction that begins with a striking statement:

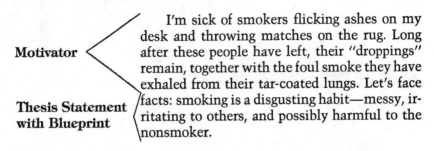

Motivator

Thesis Statement with Blueprint

I'm sick of smokers flicking ashes on my desk and throwing matches on the rug. Long after these people have left, their "droppings" remain, together with the foul smoke they have exhaled from their tar-coated lungs. Let's face facts: smoking is a disgusting habit—messy, irritating to others, and possibly harmful to the nonsmoker.

The next example of a striking statement is only two sentences long, demonstrating that an introduction can be both complete and effective even though it is fairly short. But don't use this introduction as an excuse for making all your introductions only a sentence or two long.

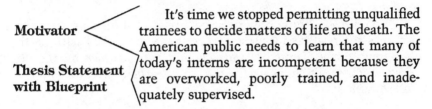

Motivator

Thesis Statement with Blueprint

It's time we stopped permitting unqualified trainees to decide matters of life and death. The American public needs to learn that many of today's interns are incompetent because they are overworked, poorly trained, and inadequately supervised.

When you are writing the introduction to your theme—whether you choose the contrary opinion, the striking incident, or the striking statement as your motivator—be sure to fulfill the two important purposes of all introductions: interest the reader, and tell him the main idea of the theme and how you will develop it.

EXERCISES

A. In Exercise A for Chapter 9 ("Thesis Statement with Blueprint"), you wrote five thesis statements with blueprints. Choose one and write an introduction that begins with the contrary opinion; choose another and write an introduction that begins with a striking incident; choose a third and write an introduction that begins with a striking statement.

B. For Exercise C in Chapter 10, you wrote a thesis statement with blueprint followed by three central paragraphs. Now, using any one of the motivators discussed in this chapter, write a full-length introduction. You may need to change the wording of the original thesis statement with blueprint for it to fit smoothly with your motivator, but do not change its essential meaning.

CHAPTER 12

Conclusion

The conclusion, like the introduction, serves two purposes: it reminds the reader of the main point of the theme, and it gives the reader a sense of finality, so that he does not turn the page and expect to find more of your essay. The part that reminds the reader of the main point of the essay is the *reworded thesis statement;* the part that gives finality is the *clincher.*

You already know how to write a reworded thesis statement: it resembles the reworded topic sentence that you worked with on the one-paragraph essay. Therefore, this chapter concentrates on the clincher. Two effective clinchers are the *reference to the motivator* and the *striking statement.*

CONCLUSION

> **Reworded Thesis Statement**
> **Clincher:** reference to the motivator or striking statement

REFERENCE TO THE MOTIVATOR

The simplest clincher reminds us of the motivator in the introduction. This clincher has the advantage of bringing the theme full circle, an unmistakable signal that the theme is over.

The preceding chapter presented three sample introductions with the thesis that smoking is disgusting. Here are those introductions again, each followed by a conclusion that refers to the motivator:

INTRODUCTION

Some people think that smoking makes them appear sophisticated and mysterious, perhaps even seductive. They become Humphrey Bogart in *Casablanca* or Lauren Bacall in *To Have and Have Not.* Those people, however, are wrong. Smoking is really a disgusting habit

—messy, irritating to others, and possibly harmful to the nonsmoker.

CONCLUSION

Reworded Thesis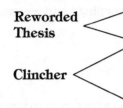

Clincher

I am glad I never began such a disgusting habit, and I wish others had not started either. I hope my "sophisticated" friends soon find out that Humphrey Bogart and Lauren Bacall were mysterious and appealing in spite of their nasty habit, not because of it.

INTRODUCTION

I walked into the living room, turned on the television, and settled back comfortably into my recliner. When the picture finally came on the screen, I was confronted by a sensuous blonde slinking toward me, her eyes looking straight into mine. She whispered provocatively, "I like a Marlboro man." I was ready to start smoking. I never did, though, because, blondes and Marlboro men notwithstanding, smoking is a disgusting habit—messy, irritating to others, and possibly harmful to the nonsmoker.

CONCLUSION

Reworded Thesis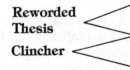

Clincher

I am glad I never began such a disgusting habit, and I wish others had not started either. My sexy blonde is no longer on television. Even though I miss her, I've never missed cigarettes.

INTRODUCTION

I'm sick of smokers flicking ashes on my desk and throwing matches on the rug. Long after these people have left, their "droppings" remain, together with the foul smoke they have exhaled from their tar-coated lungs. Let's face facts: smoking is a disgusting habit—messy, irritating to others, and possibly harmful to the nonsmoker.

CONCLUSION

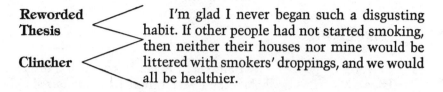

Reworded Thesis — I'm glad I never began such a disgusting habit. If other people had not started smoking, then neither their houses nor mine would be Clincher — littered with smokers' droppings, and we would all be healthier.

STRIKING STATEMENT

The last chapter presented the striking statement as a good way to begin a theme; it is also a good way to end one. Just be sure that your striking statement is clearly related to your thesis statement and is not itself a new and unproved thesis. Here is a conclusion that ends with a striking statement:

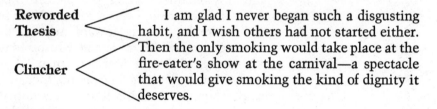

Reworded Thesis — I am glad I never began such a disgusting habit, and I wish others had not started either. Then the only smoking would take place at the fire-eater's show at the carnival—a spectacle Clincher — that would give smoking the kind of dignity it deserves.

You can find another example of the striking statement as the clincher in the sample theme in Chapter 8.

EXERCISES

A. Chapter 11 presents three introductions to a theme that shows interns are incompetent. Using the *reference to the motivator* as the clincher, write a conclusion to each one. Then, using the *striking statement* as a clincher, write a fourth conclusion to that theme.

B. For Exercise B in Chapter 11, you wrote an introduction to the three central paragraphs you had written for Chapter 10. Now complete your theme by writing the conclusion. Use either type of clincher.

CHECKLIST FOR THE FIVE-PARAGRAPH ESSAY

INTRODUCTION

_____ Does the introduction begin with a motivator?

_____ Does the introduction contain a thesis statement with blueprint?

_____ Does the thesis statement have a limited subject?

_____ Does the thesis statement have a precise opinion?

_____ Are the items in the blueprint in the same order as the paragraphs in the essay?

_____ Do the items in the blueprint all answer the same question of "Why?," "How?," or "When?"

CENTRAL PARAGRAPHS

_____ Does each central paragraph begin with a topic sentence?

_____ Does each topic sentence contain a transition from the previous paragraph?

_____ Does each topic sentence contain a reminder of the thesis statement?

_____ Does each topic sentence state the main idea of the paragraph?

_____ Is the support specific enough to be convincing?

_____ Do the items of support clearly prove the topic sentence (unity)?

_____ Do you explain your support fully so that the relation to the topic sentence is clear (coherence)?

_____ Does each item of support include a reminder of the opinion in the topic sentence (coherence)?

_____ Do you have transitions within each paragraph at the critical locations (coherence)?

CONCLUSION

_____ Does the conclusion contain a reworded thesis statement?

_____ Does the conclusion end with a clincher?

OTHER

_____ Is the essay convincing?

_____ Is the essay interesting?

_____ Are the words precise and colorful?

_____ Are grammar and sentence structure correct?

_____ Are all the words spelled correctly?

_____ Is the paper neat?

section TWO

beyond the model essay

PART IV

MORE PATTERNS OF DEVELOPMENT

In Part III you began your transition to the research paper by learning both how to write longer papers and how to use a simple method of documentation. You'll continue the transition here, again learning two important skills. First, you'll examine four different methods of developing a paper: comparison and contrast, classification, cause and effect, and process. You may discover that you have been using some of these methods already, but now you can study how they work and learn how to avoid possible pitfalls. The second skill you'll learn in this part is how to vary from the model five-paragraph essay that you've just learned. In each of the following four chapters, our sample theme differs slightly from our earlier model. At the end of each chapter, we point out and explain those differences.

CHAPTER 13

Comparison and Contrast

Comparison and contrast aren't new to you; they are extremely common ways of thinking. Whenever you examine how things are similar, you compare them, and when you look at their differences, you contrast them. Sometimes you use comparison and contrast to talk about something new: by telling your reader how a thing is similar to or different from something he knows, you can help him understand the new thing. For instance, to explain a rotary automobile engine, you'd probably compare and contrast it to the conventional automobile engine. However, besides explaining something new, comparison and contrast also appear frequently in decision-making: because A and B share some characteristics but differ in others, one is better. You compare and contrast brands when you shop for groceries, stereos, automobiles, and so forth. When you chose the college you're attending, you probably compared and contrasted available schools, and you're likely to use comparison and contrast again when you choose your major. The list of examples could be endless. The comparison-and-contrast theme, then, is really quite practical.

THESIS

Comparison and contrast lead logically to a thesis because you usually won't bother to compare and contrast unless you have some purpose in mind. You could, of course, stop once you note that A is like B or C is different from D. But your reader will probably want to know what the similarity or difference amounts to. You could write this for a thesis:

> The rotary automobile engine is different from the conventional automobile engine.

However, once you've noted the differences, the reader will see that you've merely stated the obvious. Much more useful would be one of the following:

Although the mechanical structure of the rotary automobile engine is obviously different from that of the conventional automobile engine, the rotary engine offers little worthwhile improvement.

OR

Although they both depend on internal combustion, the rotary automobile engine is a significant improvement over the conventional automobile engine.

Thus, comparison or contrast for its own sake is generally pointless, but both are extremely useful to develop support for a thesis.

APPROACHES TO COMPARISON AND CONTRAST

As you may have noticed in the preceding sample thesis statements, there are two general approaches to the comparison-and-contrast paper. First, you can note the difference between items but *concentrate on their similarity* (comparison).

Although the mechanical structure of the rotary automobile engine is obviously different from that of the conventional automobile engine, the rotary engine offers little worthwhile improvement.

Here the writer acknowledges that the engine types are different. Does the difference mean that the newer one—the rotary engine—is better? The writer says it isn't; the engines are really comparable. We can expect the theme to concentrate on the similarities of the engines.

For the second approach you can note the similarity between items but *concentrate on their difference* (contrast).

Although they both depend on internal combustion, the rotary automobile engine is a significant improvement over the conventional automobile engine.

Now the writer acknowledges one similarity—that the two engines have the same type of combustion—but he is concerned with showing that the rotary engine is better than the conventional engine.

Notice that with either similarity or difference you acknowledge the opposite. Why? You need to establish a reason for bringing items together. Noting that items seem different gives you a reason for comparing them, and noting that items appear to be similar establishes a reason for contrasting them. In both cases the opposite can provide the motivator section of your theme's introduction.

At the same time, you must decide where in the theme you're going to discuss the similarities and differences. The thesis establishes your primary purpose, which you'll concentrate on; you'll obviously discuss that side in the central paragraphs. Yet how will you deal with the opposite? You have two choices. If the opposite is well known, let the introduction handle it. But if the opposite is not generally understood, you may need to develop it in the body of the theme. In that case, cover it *first* in your central paragraphs. Doing it this way leaves the primary idea in the position of emphasis, the end of the theme.

CENTRAL PARAGRAPH ORGANIZATION

When you've decided whether to concentrate on comparison or contrast, you still must decide how to do it. Suppose you want to contrast two brands of automobile to decide which to buy; you'll consider such subtopics as price, miles per gallon, and maintenance record. You must decide whether to devote the central paragraphs to whole items (the cars) or to their various elements (price, miles per gallon, and maintenance record). The chart shows the two most likely organizational types (we've used two items with three elements per item, but other combinations are certainly possible):

TYPE I	TYPE II
Introduction	Introduction
Item A Element 1 Element 2 Element 3	**Element 1** Item A Item B
Item B Element 1 Element 2 Element 3	**Element 2** Item A Item B
	Element 3 Item A Item B
Conclusion	Conclusion

Whether you choose the Type I or Type II organization for the central paragraphs of your theme, make sure that you always cover the same subtopics in the same order. As with parallelism within a sentence (see Chapter 32), this paragraphing symmetry will clearly show the relationships that are important for your ideas.

Which pattern is preferable? Well, notice that the Type I organization gives a sense of each item as a whole; however, the reader may have difficulty relating the elements. For example, suppose you compare a Datsun and a Toyota on the basis of seven elements. By the time the reader gets to element five of the second car, the Toyota, he's forgotten what he read about element five of the Datsun. As a result, Type I organization is better for short papers dealing with only a few items and elements. On the other hand, Type II organization destroys the sense of the whole item as it builds the relationships of the elements. Still, Type II development can handle more items and more elements, so it's more useful than Type I for a longer comparison or contrast paper. So which type is better? There's no absolute answer, but you'll see more papers using Type II organization, probably because people are more concerned with element-by-element similarities and differences.

Here's a sample theme that compares two characters in literature. We've selected this theme because English instructors often ask you to write about literature; as you'll see, a theme comparing two fictional characters is fairly easy to organize. You'll also see how well the Type II organization works for comparing a large number of subtopic elements, even though there are only two items.

Holmes and Dupin

Although Sir Arthur Conan Doyle created Sherlock Holmes in 1886, Holmes remains one of the most popular of detective characters. Moreover, Holmes' personality influenced the characterizations of other fictional detectives, both in Doyle's time and later. For example, Agatha Christie's Hercule Poirot is similar to Holmes. Yet many readers of the Holmes stories don't realize that Holmes isn't entirely original. Holmes is very much like Chevalier C. Auguste Dupin, a character Edgar Allan Poe introduced in 1841. Of course, Holmes and Dupin have their differences; Holmes himself calls Dupin "a very inferior fellow" (Doyle, *A Study in Scarlet and The Sign of Four*, p. 25). Nevertheless, pushing aside Holmes' criticism of Dupin, we can find numerous similarities between the two characters. Both in professional situation and in personality, Holmes is a copy of Dupin.

The conditions under which Dupin and Holmes work are alike. Both Dupin and Holmes are "consulting detectives," to use Holmes' name for the profession (Doyle, p. 23). This may not seem important, but we should notice that most other detective characters take cases on their own. On the other hand, Dupin works on cases for Monsieur G——, Prefect of the Parisian police, and Holmes (at least when he first appears) works on cases that have stumped Scotland Yard detectives. In addition, both characters dislike the policemen they work for, and for the same reason. In "The Purloined Letter" Dupin says that the police are "persevering, ingenious, cunning, and thoroughly versed in the knowledge which their duties seem chiefly to demand" but that they fail because they cannot adapt their methods "to the case and to the man" (Poe, *Great Tales and Poems of Edgar Allan Poe*, pp. 208–209). Similarly, Holmes says the Scotland Yard detectives are "both quick and energetic, but conventional—shockingly so" (Doyle, p. 28). Still, Dupin and Holmes somehow control their scorn while they solve cases for the police. The "consulting detectives" have the satisfaction of solving puzzles, but let the police steal the glory.

Holmes' personality also matches Dupin's. Both characters are loners; they accept the company of the narrators of their stories, but of no one else. Poe writes in "The Murders in the Rue Morgue" that Dupin is "enamored of the night for her own sake"; in fact, Dupin and the narrator close the shutters of their house during the day and usually go out only at night (Poe, pp. 106–107). This love of darkness emphasizes Dupin's physical withdrawal from society. In Holmes' case, the withdrawal and gloominess lead to cocaine addiction; when Holmes isn't on a case, he withdraws from ordinary life as well as from society. Of course, the detectives become active in society to solve cases, but each withdraws again when his case is over. At the opening of the second Dupin story, the narrator says that after his first case Dupin "relapsed into his old habits of moody revery" (Poe, p. 144). And Holmes at the end of *The Sign of Four* calls for his cocaine so he, too, can withdraw.

Even when Dupin and Holmes actually enter society to solve puzzles, they remain mentally separate from other men. On a case, both Dupin and Holmes show energy unknown to most people. This energy involves them in society, but it doesn't mean that they actually join society. Instead, each stays separate by remaining unemotional; unlike ordinary men, they appear to be minds without feelings. In "The Murders in the Rue Morgue" the narrator describes the working Dupin as "frigid and abstract," with eyes "vacant in expression" (Poe, p. 107). Doyle is more obvious about Holmes. In *The Sign of Four* Holmes says that "detection is, or ought to be, an exact science and should be treated in the same cold and unemotional manner" (Doyle, p. 137). Like Dupin, then, Holmes prefers to have a mind free of emotions.

Thus, the number of similarities between the two characters shows that the 1886 Holmes is a copy of the 1841 Dupin. They take their cases for the same reason and handle them with the same dislike for their police associates. Neither character can stand the world of normal men, choosing instead to withdraw into a secret shell. And even when they work with ordinary men, they remain aloof, emotionless. These similarities are too numerous to be accidental. Clearly Doyle owes a large debt to Poe.

VARYING FROM THE MODEL THEME

As you read in the introduction to Part IV, the sample themes in this set of chapters will sometimes vary from the model five-paragraph essay. Did you see the differences in the essay for this chapter?

First, the paragraph divisions are different from what you may have expected after you read the essay's introduction. The blueprint shows only two topic divisions, but the essay uses three central paragraphs. You might have expected this organization:

Introduction

Similarities in "Professional Situation"

Similarities in "Personality"

Conclusion

You saw this instead:

Introduction

Similarities in "Professional Situation"

Similarities in "Personality"

Similarities in "Personality" (continued)

Conclusion

Because he had too much to discuss in one paragraph per major topic, the writer broke up the second topic into two logical groups. Thus, what began in his mind as a four-paragraph essay became (out of necessity) a five-paragraph essay.

Second, the topic sentences do not always fit exactly the model you studied earlier. The topic sentences of paragraphs two and three connect directly to the thesis. These two topic sentences begin major divisions of the support, so their topic ideas are vital for the thesis. However, paragraph four merely continues the idea of the previous paragraph. Therefore, the topic sentence contains a transition and the main idea of the paragraph, but not a reminder of the thesis.

Still, it is worth noting that the writer *could* have strictly followed the model for the multiparagraph essay. Why didn't he? He didn't need to. You, too, have developed in your writing skills; your judgment about writing has also developed. You are moving beyond simple topics dealing with only your experiences and imagination; you can also move beyond the model essay. But as the sample theme for this chapter shows, the general idea of the model can help you handle a sophisticated topic. Therefore, let the needs of your topic determine the final pattern of your essay, but keep the model in your mind as a ready—and effective—guide.

EXERCISES

A. For each of the two topics below, first limit the topic and then write *two* thesis statements, one for each approach to a comparison-and-contrast paper.

Example: Topic: Automobile

Limited topic: _____ Engine types _____

Acknowledge the difference and concentrate on the simi-

larity: Although the mechanical structure of the rotary

automobile engine is obviously different from that of the

conventional automobile engine, the rotary engine offers

little worthwhile improvement.

_____

Acknowledge the similarity and concentrate on the differ-

ence: Although they both depend on internal combus-

tion, the rotary automobile engine is a significant improve-

ment over the conventional automobile engine.

_____

1. Topic: Sports

   Limited topic: _____

   Acknowledge the difference and concentrate on the similarity: _____

   _____

   _____

   _____

   _____

   _____

   Acknowledge the similarity and concentrate on the difference: _____

   _____

   _____

   _____

   _____

   _____

2. Topic: Emotions

   Limited topic: _____

   Acknowledge the difference and concentrate on the similarity: _____

   _____

   _____

   _____

   _____

   Acknowledge the similarity and concentrate on the difference: _____

   _____

   _____

   _____

   _____

   _____

B. Choose one of the thesis statements you developed for Exercise A and outline the central paragraphs for a theme to support the thesis. Make your outline conform to either the Type I or the Type II central paragraph organization: for each central paragraph you will need to show a topic item with subtopic elements (Type I) or a topic element with subtopic items (Type II).

C. Here are some possible topics for comparison-and-contrast papers:

Animals	Movies
Athletes	Music
Commercial Products	Relatives or Friends
Literature	Television

First limit the topic; then write a thesis that concentrates on comparison or contrast. Organize your support with the Type I or Type II pattern, and then write the theme. If you wish to vary from the model theme, do so, but list your variations on a separate page at the end of your paper. And if you use outside sources for support, be sure to document them (you can use the makeshift system, as the sample theme in the chapter does).

CHAPTER 14

Classification

Often we find ourselves with a long list of items we'd like to talk about but with no simple way to discuss them. We do know we could handle the items if we put them into three or four groups. This process of grouping a long list into categories is *classification*.

Consider this example. At the end of classes on Friday you look for a way to tackle all the studying you need to do over the weekend. Some of the work is so simple that you can do it right away before you go to a movie. You want to save some of the assignments for Sunday so the lessons will be fresh in your mind on Monday morning. And there are a couple of small research projects that would be good for a library session on Saturday. To cope with the amount of studying you have to do, you classify the assignments under these headings:

Things to Study Friday

Things to Study Saturday

Things to Study Sunday

Now you've reduced a long list to three groups. But the important idea is that the groups all answer the same question: When is a good time to do this work? In other words, you've classified according to *one* characteristic related to all the items in the list.

If you classify on the basis of a different characteristic related to the items, you'll get a different listing. For example, as usual you don't study as hard over the weekend as you planned to on Friday afternoon; late Sunday night you find yourself with most of the work still to do. Perhaps you make a new list, like this:

Put Off Until Next Weekend

Put Off Until Final Exams

Put Off Forever

Now the groupings are based on how long you can avoid doing the work, so this listing will not be identical with the one you made on Friday afternoon.

Dozens of times each week we organize items by classification. We classify when we sort laundry into piles for machine wash, hand wash, or dry clean; or when we put the machine wash into piles for hot water, cold water, or medium temperature. We think of automobiles in groupings: by size (subcompact, compact, intermediate, and so on), by cost (under $6000, $6000 to $8000, and so on), or by expected use (individual, family, or commercial). Because classification is such a common way of thinking, it is also a popular type of theme development. The groupings automatically provide us with the theme's *organization* and help us see what we want to say about the groups, our *thesis*.

ORGANIZATION

Since it breaks a topic into packages, classification results in a simple pattern that matches the model for the multiparagraph essay. Each category forms a central paragraph:

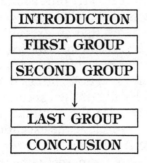

You'll see a theme using a pattern similar to this one later in the chapter.

Yet, easy as the pattern of development is, you need to avoid its three potential pitfalls. You can tumble into any one of them if you're not careful when you classify.

The first problem is limiting the subject you intend to classify. A subject that is too broad could contain hundreds of items. You could put these hundreds into two or three groups, but the groups probably wouldn't be useful since each would still include a long list of items. On the other hand, you could classify hundreds of items into a large number of groups (say fifteen), but then you'd have to write a theme with fifteen central paragraphs. In either case you might as well not classify. Instead, limit the subject until it includes a workable number of items. For example, you choose "Ethnic Groups" as your subject. The world has too many ethnic groups for you to work with. You limit to "Major Ethnic Groups in the United States," but the number of items still seems endless. Limiting the subject to "Major Ethnic Groups in San Francisco" should solve the problem.

The second and most common problem is related to unity. Remember that to classify is to group on the basis of *one* characteristic related to each item. If more than one kind of grouping shows up in your theme, you've failed to maintain unity; and a reader who is troubled by the groupings themselves probably will not be convinced by your argument. Consider this list of categories for types of car:

American	Italian
Japanese	Luxury
German	

"Luxury" is not a country of origin. The grouping is unacceptable.

Finally, you need to realize that many classifications that work well for grouping items actually have minor flaws. For instance, we often put motorized passenger vehicles that run on land into three convenient groups: cars, trucks, and buses. Yet this classification does not cover the special vehicle that looks like a large station wagon (a car) but is built on a truck chassis (a truck) and can carry nine adults (a small bus). There's no simple rule for dealing with this problem; however, there is a reasonable procedure to follow when you find an exception to your classes. First, judge the importance of the exception. If the exception destroys the point you are trying to make (the thesis of your argument), then rethink your groupings. And if a "single exception" brings to mind dozens more, then again you must regroup. Finally, if the exception remains a minor flaw, you may want to acknowledge the complication somewhere in your paper. Or you may be able to exclude the exceptions by the way you word your subject. For example, if you write about "Religions on My Campus," you'll have to deal with all of them, including that of the single student who has made an idol of the oak tree on the campus mall, but if you write about "Major Religions on My Campus," you've eliminated the minor exceptions to your categories.

THESIS

Classification leads logically to one of two types of thesis. The classification may itself be the thesis. Or the classification may be only the means of organizing the argument that persuades the reader to accept a thesis. The first is easier to write, but the second generally makes a better theme.

If your classification reveals striking groupings, the classification itself may be the thesis. Such a thesis takes the general form of "There are (*number of groups*) for (*topic*)." For example, "There are three types of teacher," or "There are two types of politician." Not very interesting, really. Still, sometimes the groupings themselves reveal your stand on the topic. Then the "there are" thesis may work. Consider this example:

> Today there are two types of politician: the dishonest and the half-honest.

Implicit in these classes is the thesis that no politician today is completely honest.

Often, however, the "there are" thesis is not satisfying by itself. The reader yawns and mutters "So what?" What the reader is really asking is why the writer bothered to classify items. Consider this thesis:

> There are four types of door lock available for home use.

If the reader happens to be interested in locks, the thesis may work. Probably more interesting would be a theme that uses the types of door lock to make a more important point, such as this:

> Although there are four types of door lock available for home use, an expert burglar can fool any of them.

Now the thesis is that the locks are not foolproof; the writer will develop his theme with a central paragraph for each type of lock, but he'll be showing in each case that the locks will not stop a determined burglar.

When you develop a subject by classification, you'll have to judge the value of your classification. Will the reader care that you've identified groups? Or do the groups merely help reveal something more important?

Here's a sample theme (a four-paragraph essay) in which classification serves as an organizational stepping-stone to get to the thesis idea.

The Waistland of TV Advertisements

Like thousands of Americans, my compulsive drive to eat keeps me continually on a diet. When I told a friend that I eat if I'm happy, sad, or just sort of blah, he said I need to occupy my mind. He suggested that when I'm hungry I should watch television. This solution seemed particularly appropriate, for I enjoy television when I'm happy, when I'm sad, and when my mind is too dull to feel much of anything. My friend was right about the television shows; even the worst of them draws my attention away from food. But my friend forgot about the advertisements. Whether commercials for food in restaurants or for food to take home, these television advertisements represent cruel and all-too-usual punishment for the dieter.

Numerous restaurant ads provide seemingly continuous reminders of a world of eating enjoyment, all of it forbidden on my 1200-calorie diet. There are so many restaurant ads that I can turn from channel to channel during commercial time and usually be assaulted with only one laundry-detergent ad, one pet-food ad, but four ads for restaurants. After a week on my diet, I'm jealous of the kitten in the cat chow commercial; imagine what the barrage of restaurant ads does to me. There are commercials for steak (with salad, potato, and toast), pizza (thick or thin crust, with dozens of toppings to choose from), fish or clams, chicken (with fixin's), hamburgers (with or without cheese, decorated with catsup and mustard, sprinkled with chopped onions and lettuce, topped with a pickle, stuffed in a lightly toasted bun), roast beef or ham sandwiches (for a change from the hamburger habit), and tacos or burritos (as well as related Mexican foods that I've never heard of but begin to crave anyway when I see them on TV). Need I go on? Probably by now even your stomach has started to rumble, and you've had more for supper than my spoonful of cottage cheese on half a small peach (made more appetizing by a scrap of wilting lettuce for decoration).

Less numerous than restaurant ads but more enticing are the commercials for the foods I can buy to take home. When I've been starved for carbohydrates for a few days, the convenience of the take-home foods appeals to the remnants of my ability to reason. You see, if my willpower wavers and I go to a restaurant—even a quick-order place—someone who knows I'm dieting may catch me, but it's easy to dart into a grocery store, ice-cream parlor, or doughnut shop and dash home without being seen. Besides, the TV ads for foods to take home are so inviting. For example, you may remember seeing the advertisement for one of the doughnut shops in town. As the TV camera pans slowly across a counter laden with bakery goodies, I begin to drool. The commercial's soundtrack broadcasts a man calling to his wife to run to the TV to see the panorama of food laid out before his—and my—impressionable eyes. He says that the sight of the doughnuts will "drive him crazy," and his voice sounds as though he's already slightly deranged because of what he sees. He proclaims the scene "heavenly," but I know it's a dieter's hell. I've always assumed he demands that his wife give him her car keys so he can rush to the doughnut shop; I say "assumed" because I've never stayed at my TV set long enough to hear the end of the commercial. I'm on my way out the door to beat that crazy fool to the best of the doughnuts.

You're reading the rantings of a dieter too often distracted by hunger and too long provoked by TV commercials for food. Yes, I confess—stop the torture—the ads are obviously effective. I salivate right on cue for all the food advertisers. But in my few remaining rational moments I can still judge those advertisements for restaurants and take-home foods. To the dieter they're cruel. They play on the dieter's weakness, his compulsion to eat. But I'll have my revenge, in my own limited way. My friend has invited me to his apartment tomorrow to watch TV, as he puts it, "to relieve the depression" of my latest diet. I'll sit calmly in his favorite chair; I'll stare innocently at his television. But when the first commercial for food comes on, I'm going to cut the plug off his set. While he's paralyzed by shock, I'll go into his kitchen to make myself a sandwich.

Don't be fooled by this writer's pretension of insanity; behind the writer's mask is a pattern of development dependent upon classification. Because he recognizes that there are too many different food ads to deal with individually, the writer has classified them into two groups—foods to eat in restaurants and foods to eat at home. Are you bothered by the fact that some of the foods he classes as restaurant foods could be taken home? Probably not, because the inconsistency will not damage his thesis. And besides, for him the classification may well be valid; some types of foods he consistently eats at restaurants (though he could take them home) and some types he buys for his pantry. What we should recognize is this: classifications are arbitrary, but they do allow us a reasonable means to organize material. All in all, the classification in this theme is reasonable. It allows the writer to package his support material so that he can get to his thesis.

VARYING FROM THE MODEL THEME

Did you notice the minor differences in the sample theme for this chapter? For one, the thesis is not a simple statement of "limited subject is precise opinion," but we could still tell that the writer would need to show that the food ads are numerous and that they are "cruel." You may have noticed that the first central paragraph is the Stage I type, whereas the second central paragraph, which uses subtopic sentences, is a Stage II type. Finally, in the conclusion no single sentence fully restates the thesis; nevertheless, the first five sentences of the conclusion as a whole do remind us of the thesis. As you can see, the general pattern of the multiparagraph essay remains, even though there are deviations from the model.

EXERCISES

A. Circle the class in each list below that breaks the unity of the classification.

    1. Topic: Automobiles
        Classes: Ford
                Chevrolet
                Datsun
                Capri
    2. Topic: Football players
        Classes: quarterbacks
                ends
                triple-options
                halfbacks
    3. Topic: Schools
        Classes: elementary
                junior high
                year-round
                high school
                college
    4. Topic: Foods
        Classes: fruits
                vegetables
                peaches
                meats

B. Each subject below is too broad to classify easily. First limit the subject and then name at least three classes.

    Example: Topic: Television
           Limited topic: daytime television shows
        Classes: soap operas
                   game shows
                   talk shows
                   news programs

    1. Topic: Jobs

        Limited topic: _____

        Classes: _____

_____

_____

_____

_____

2. Topic: Books

    Limited topic: _____

    Classes: _____

    _____

    _____

    _____

    _____

3. Topic: Clothes

    Limited topic: _____

    Classes: _____

    _____

    _____

    _____

    _____

4. Topic: Advertising

    Limited topic: _____

    Classes: _____

    _____

    _____

    _____

    _____

C.   In Exercise B you classified four limited topics. Choose one that interests you and write a multiparagraph essay that you organize by classification. Remember that you can make your theme more interesting if you use classification to develop a thesis other than the classification itself.

D.   Use classification to develop a multiparagraph essay about one of the following topics. You'll need to limit the topic before you attempt to classify it, just as you did in Exercise B.

Emotions
Relatives
Television
Religion
Politics

If you wish to vary from the model theme, do so, but list your variations on a separate page at the end of your paper. If you use outside sources for support, be sure to document them. You can use the makeshift system you learned in Part III.

CHAPTER 15

Cause and Effect

Remember the "Why?" subtopic sentences you studied in Chapter 7? Maybe you didn't realize it at the time, but you were studying one kind of cause-and-effect paper. We'll examine cause-effect papers more closely in this chapter.

A *cause* is a reason something happens; an *effect*, then, is whatever happens. As a simple example, we might say, "Because the television set is unplugged, it doesn't work." The *cause* is that the set is unplugged; the *effect* is that the set doesn't work.

You can write three kinds of cause-effect papers: you can state that the effect is true and examine the *cause* in detail; you can state that the cause is true and examine the *effect* in detail; or you can attempt to show that the *entire cause-effect statement* is true.

EXAMINING THE CAUSES

Sometimes the controversial part of a cause-effect statement is the cause, so your paper will naturally examine that part in detail. Let's say you've decided to write about this thesis: "The aggravated assault rate here at Gila Monster Maximum Security Prison has decreased dramatically because of the warden's innovations." The effect—that the aggravated assault rate has dropped—shouldn't be controversial, so take care of that part quickly with a statistic or two in your introduction: "In the last year, the aggravated assault rate at Gila Monster Maximum Security Prison has plummeted from nineteen per month to only four per month." After dispensing with the effect, spend the rest of your paper telling us about the warden's policies and why they work.

How? Write a paragraph about each of the warden's important policies. Your outline might look something like this:

Thesis: Because of the warden's innovations, the aggravated assault rate at Gila Monster Maximum Security Prison has decreased dramatically.

Topic Sentence: The warden's new leathercraft shop allows inmates a constructive way to spend their time.

Topic Sentence: The warden has started an intramural sports program that permits the prisoners a physical outlet for their pent-up emotions.

Topic Sentence: The new co-ed jail cells allow the inmates the chance to discuss relevant social issues with members of the opposite sex.

Of course, you don't need to have exactly three central paragraphs. Two especially well-developed paragraphs or four or five shorter ones could work also.

EXAMINING THE EFFECTS

Sometimes the cause is fairly straightforward, but the effect needs elaboration. What if your thesis is that "Because Napoleon's wars killed many young men who otherwise could have worked a lifetime, Europe's standard of living dropped markedly"? Not many people would doubt that the wars killed many young men who could have done a lot of work, but people still might doubt that the standard of living actually did drop. You need to state the cause as a fact and then elaborate upon the effect.

You could then begin the theme by mentioning in the introduction (perhaps using the "striking statement" motivator) how many young men were slaughtered. Then you could develop the theme by discussing the effect ("Europe's standard of living dropped markedly") in three or four European countries. Here's a possible outline:

Thesis: Because Napoleon's wars killed many young men who otherwise could have worked a lifetime, Europe's standard of living dropped markedly.

Topic Sentence: After Napoleon's wars, Russia had a lower standard of living.

Topic Sentence: Austria also had a lower standard of living.

Topic Sentence: Even Napoleon's home, France, had a lower standard of living.

EXAMINING THE ENTIRE CAUSE-EFFECT STATEMENT

Sometimes the cause-effect papers examine the entire statement instead of only half of it. Perhaps both cause and effect are controversial, or perhaps neither is controversial but the fact that they have a cause-effect relationship is.

Let's look first at a cause-effect statement in which both parts are controversial and need elaboration. What if we say that "Because Colorado land developers have no long-term stake in the development they sell, customers often end up with property they cannot inhabit"? We'll have to persuade the reader of two ideas: that the developers do not have any long-term interests in development and that the new landowners can't live on their property. Both parts need support.

One simple way to organize the support is to write a paragraph on the cause and a paragraph on the effect. We could show in the first central paragraph that Colorado developers do not have any long-term interest in the land; in the next paragraph, then, we could show that the new owners often cannot use their property.

However, we could probably write a better paper by examining both parts of the cause-effect statement in the same paragraph. How? We could use examples. We'll make each central paragraph a narrative example of the entire cause-effect statement. One paragraph might be about Pyrite Acres, a development bulldozed out of the desert at the base of the Sangre de Cristo mountains. The developer, after selling the last site, disappeared into Arizona with all the money. He had not found time to tell the new owners that the underground water supply was so low that it could last for only another year or two. Then—if our thesis is really valid—we should be able to present a paragraph on each of two or three similar situations with other developers. Extended examples can be effective any time both the cause and the effect need support.

Extended examples can help in another case, the one in which both the cause and the effect are fairly straightforward, but their relationship is not. Consider this statement: "Because many mountain climbers are elated after a difficult climb, they are in danger from carelessness after the difficulty is past." We can accept easily that climbers are elated after a difficult ascent; we can accept also that climbers who are careless afterward are in danger. We would probably like to see support for the idea that the elation from a difficult climb produces that carelessness. The following sample theme uses extended examples to provide such support. As you read this theme, you might also try to discover how it differs from the model for a five-paragraph essay we presented in Part III. We'll come back to this point at the end of the chapter.

The Matterhorn Effect

Only a little over a century ago, some people in Europe thought that the Matterhorn—that awesome, beautiful pinnacle— was the highest mountain in the world. Many climbers from many nations had raced to climb it, but none had succeeded. Then in 1865, an Englishman, Edward Whymper, and six others reached the summit, but only Whymper and two others lived to tell about it. The rest, careless from elation and fatigue, died when one climber slipped on a relatively easy part of the descent and carried three others over a 4000-foot cliff. That carelessness, a mental letdown that climbers tend to experience after succeeding at something hard, is called the "Matterhorn effect." I've seen it myself.

I remember how pleased I was when I first climbed Borderline, a hard route up a 150-foot spire in the Garden of the Gods, Colorado. Only six others had ever climbed it. My forearms were so cramped from exertion that I could barely pull the rope up as my climbing partner, Leonard Coyne, seconded the route. After reaching the top, Leonard mentioned that he knew the descent route was fairly hard, though the previous climbers had disdained using a rope for it. Filled with overconfidence, I simply tossed the rope to the ground below. We had just done the tough ascent, so surely we did not need a rope either. Then I started down the nearly vertical face. Suddenly Leonard yelled, "Your handhold is loose! Grab my leg!" There I was—unroped, 150 feet above the ground, and apprehensively holding a couple of loose flakes of rock—when my *foothold* broke. I still don't know what kept me on the rock, but apparently as my foothold gave way, my foot slipped onto a barely visible toehold. I didn't fall, but if I hadn't been overconfident from the hard ascent, I would never have ventured into that dangerous position without a rope.

I've seen the Matterhorn effect almost claim Leonard, too. Last summer, he, Gary Campbell, and I had just finished climbing the northwest face of Half Dome, a magnificent 2000-foot vertical cliff in Yosemite, California. We'd been climbing, eating, and sleeping on the face for three days, and finally we were on top—well, almost. Actually, we were about 30 feet from the top, but that part was really easy. We untied, coiled the ropes, and stowed our climbing hardware. Leonard slung on one of the packs—a rather unwieldy thing with a sleeping bag tied precariously to the outside—and started up the last 30 feet. As he began to haul himself onto a five-foot shelf, the pack shifted on his back, almost jerking him off the rock. Two thousand feet above the ground, he balanced—like a turtle about to flip on its back—for what seemed like a minute before he rolled slowly forward onto the shelf. Three days of numbing fatigue and the elation of doing such a hard climb had caused us all to have a mental letdown; we had put away the ropes too soon. That letdown almost cost Leonard his life.

The point is clear to me: the Matterhorn effect is real for anybody who has just done something hard, but especially for climbers. I've seen it in myself too many times and too many times in others.

But—so far, at least—I've been fortunate not to learn about it in the way Edward Whymper and his companions did.

Each extended example in this sample theme presents the entire cause-effect relationship. The cause (the author's elation and fatigue on Borderline and Leonard's on Half Dome) seems to lead quite naturally to the effect (the near-accidents).

PITFALLS OF THE CAUSE-EFFECT THEME

In the last chapter you learned not to choose a subject that is too general for your classification paper. That advice is still true for cause-effect papers. In a theme, you could never hope to convince a disbeliever of this thesis: "Because the United States wanted to insure the freedom of South Vietnam, it went to war against North Vietnam." You'd need a book, or a substantial chapter in one, to support that statement.

You must also be careful that your cause-effect statement presents the important cause and not just a secondary one. We'd be foolish to blame a field-goal kicker for losing an important game just because he missed a thirty-two yard attempt during the last five seconds. The team may have lost in part because of that missed attempt, but what about the quarterback who threw an interception during the first quarter, the defensive lineman who missed a key tackle, or the coach who canceled practice last Wednesday? Be sure, in other words, that your cause is really the main cause.

VARYING FROM THE MODEL THEME

As you saw in the last chapter, one of our purposes in Part IV is to help you learn how to vary from the model theme. How does our sample about the Matterhorn effect differ from the model five-paragraph essay you learned in Part III? Before we discuss the differences, look back at the sample in this chapter and underline the thesis, blueprint, and topic sentences. Then read on.

You probably noticed immediately that the sample has only four paragraphs. An extra central paragraph would have been too much, tacked on just to fill out the model. This theme didn't need another central paragraph for two reasons: both central paragraphs are very fully developed and—more important—the introduction contains another example already.

You probably underlined this sentence as the thesis: "That careless-ness, a mental letdown that climbers tend to experience after succeeding at something hard, is called the 'Matterhorn effect.'" It doesn't exactly state the main idea of the paper (that the Matterhorn effect is real) but certainly it implies it. Readers expect the rest of the paper to convince them that the Matterhorn effect exists.

Did you find a blueprint? The last sentence of the first paragraph—"I've seen it myself"—is not really a blueprint of the topic ideas for each paragraph, but it certainly *implies* the development. We know we are about to read some examples.

The topic sentence for the first central paragraph is also implied, not by any one sentence but by the entire paragraph. A stated topic sentence isn't nearly as important as unified support and coherence. As long as you could write a topic sentence for a paragraph—the paragraph, in other words, is unified—and as long as the reader has no doubt what he is read-ing and why, a topic sentence is not necessary.

EXERCISES

A. Use these topics to answer the items below:
      bank robbers
      childbirth in the home
      nuclear power plants
      pesticides
      obedience training for dogs
      public swimming pools
      claustrophobia

1. Write a cause-effect thesis with a cause that is controversial but an effect that isn't. Then write three proposed topic sentences to show how you could develop your thesis.

    Thesis: _____

    _____

    Topic Sentence: _____

    _____

    Topic Sentence: _____

    _____

    Topic Sentence: _____

    _____

2. Write a cause-effect thesis with an effect that is controversial

but a cause that isn't. Again write the topic sentences you would use.

Thesis: _____

_____

Topic Sentence: _____

_____

Topic Sentence: _____

_____

Topic Sentence: _____

_____

3. Write a cause-effect thesis that has both a controversial cause and a controversial effect. Write the proposed topic sentences.

Thesis: _____

_____

Topic Sentence: _____

_____

Topic Sentence: _____

_____

Topic Sentence: _____

_____

B. Find your own support and write a cause-effect theme using this thesis: "Because they try to dupe me, I object to car advertisements in magazines." Choose some other kind of advertisement if you like, but attach the advertisements to your paper when you hand it in. If you wish to vary from the model theme, do so, but list your variations on a separate page at the end of your paper.

C. Choose something that had a significant effect on you and write a cause-effect paper. Exercise B above could have been a response. Again, if you wish to vary from the model theme, list your variations on a separate page. If you use outside sources for support, be sure to document them. You can use the makeshift system you learned in Part III.

D. Choose one of the topics listed at the beginning of A (not necessarily one you outlined) and write the theme. If you wish to vary from the model theme, list your variations on a separate page. If you use outside sources for support, be sure to document them. You can use the makeshift system you learned in Part III.

CHAPTER 16

Process

A process paper describes a series of steps that leads to a result. You've used such description before—when you gave directions to the post office, or told a new student how to register, or explained how an old friend had changed. In each case you described a progression of steps.

Although we call this kind of presentation a process description, it can use all the other kinds of writing you study about in this book. If we try to explain how the United States became involved in the Panama Canal, we might use cause and effect to describe the chronological steps in the process. If we try to describe how the boy in Hemingway's *The Old Man and the Sea* changes, we might use comparison and contrast to show the process of change, his step-by-step growth. In other words, process description can use all the other modes of writing, but the key element is that process description is divided into steps: first this, then this, later this, and finally this happens.

THESIS

As in the other forms of writing, your thesis is the key to a good essay. In a process description, you might have either of two kinds of thesis: one argumentative, one informative. For example, you might say "Getting in shape by jogging benefits the body more than getting in shape by swimming." This thesis argues that jogging is better than swimming if you want to get in shape. Or you might use a purely informative thesis to explain an unfamiliar process to your readers: how to make cheese; phases in the Battle of Chickamauga; how to drive from Chicago to Memphis; how to pack a small car.

ORGANIZATION

Somewhere in the opening of your paper you must explain any unusual equipment for the process you're describing, or you must provide the necessary background information so your reader understands the significance of the process. If the equipment or background information is simple and short, put it in the introduction. But if it's detailed and lengthy, include it in a paragraph after the introduction but before the discussion paragraphs describing the process.

The key idea in a process description is to divide whatever process you're discussing into steps. (Note that a simple listing of helpful ideas probably won't show the step-by-step progression to make clear the process.) Because a process description moves from step to step, the order of ideas is always chronological, first step first, then the second step, and so on. Sometimes you will need to spend a full paragraph on each step. Other times you will need to group several small steps into a longer paragraph or two. The organization of a process description looks like this:

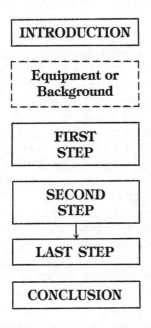

Within each step you must remember to do certain things:

1. Define new terms when they appear; use a dictionary definition or a clear comparison to something familiar that your reader will understand.
2. Include helpful hints, if appropriate to your paper.
3. Warn of dangers or possible pitfalls if you are describing a mechanical process.

Regardless of the subject of your process description, you must remember to divide it into logical, chronological steps.

Here's a sample description of a process unfamiliar to many people:

Packing a Small Car

Not so long ago packing the car for a vacation meant tossing five or six suitcases into the back of a large station wagon, with room left for the St. Bernard if Father would let the kids drag him along. For many American families today, though, packing the family car isn't such a simple process. Still, even the trunk space of a modest four-cylinder sedan will hold the luggage for a family of four if you apply common sense to the planning and preparation steps of the packing process.

Before you even begin the packing process, however, you have to judge whether the carrying space available in the car is likely to be sufficient for your needs. If you have three large boxes of presents to transport to the Christmas gathering at Grandmother's, the space in the family car may not be enough. And don't forget the return trip, because you may want to bring home more than you take away with you. There are several ways to expand upon the carrying space available: adding a cartop carrier, pulling a trailer, or even renting a truck. The point itself is simple, though. The carrying space of a small car is sufficient for the clothes and personal items for a family of four, but not for much more. And certainly the best time to realize that you need to add space is before you begin packing, not at the last minute when you're faced with leaving behind two-year-old Susie or all of Mother's clothes.

The first step in the packing process is planning what to take. The key here is to limit the desire to carry along all the comforts of home, particularly if the family is accustomed to other times with a bigger automobile. You can easily carry clothes for four people for four or five days, as long as everyone is reasonably conservative in the number of outfits selected. For a two or three week vacation, however, plan on making arrangements for doing laundry rather than on packing clothes for the whole time. Extras such as tennis rackets or golf clubs will need to be few or small. Finally, if your family is used to packing a large ice chest and a picnic basket for meals at roadside rest stops, you probably will have to learn to settle for Big Macs instead.

Once you get over the initial disappointment at not being able to take along everything you could have packed in the family's old car, you're in for a pleasant surprise—the family car of today still actually holds quite a lot. If you are to make full use of the space, however, the second stage in the packing process is crucial. In this step you select and pack the containers you'll later fit into the car. The key here is selecting medium and small containers. The beginner might try to pack everything into three or four large suitcases and boxes. After all, if the car has, say, 12 cubic feet of trunk space, it ought to hold four containers with 3 cubic feet each. That just won't work. The luggage space in today's small car, even in a small station wagon, usually is broken up, so choosing medium and small containers allows you to fit more into the car than if you had packed an equal volume in large containers. A mixture of medium and small containers will work well: two or three medium suitcases, two or three medium boxes (the 1½ cubic foot size), and the remainder in small boxes and bags. The small boxes and bags allow you to fit items into the odd-shaped spaces, while the medium containers cut down the chore of lugging packages to and from the car. You strike a balance, then, between ease of packing the car and ease of carrying.

Finally comes packing, but even this obvious step has its common sense keys. The first is to get everything in sight as you pack the car. You could fit each item into the car as you carried it outside, but the chances for frustration increase when you pack this way. You'll likely end up with items of the right volume but the wrong shape to fit the hole that's left at the end. On the other hand, if you can see everything you have to fit into the car as you're packing, you can choose more wisely from among the sizes and shapes available to you at any moment. The second key is to pack in a layered fashion. This means that you set one layer of medium-sized items in place in the car and then pack small items around them, being careful to fill every available space in that layer. Complete this first layer before you set in the second layer of medium-sized containers. Then, of course, repeat with filling in the odd-shaped spaces that remain. Finally, if you're cautious, you'll keep to the last a few of the least essential small containers to provide for a margin of error in your planning. If you simply can't fit in the last item or two, wouldn't it be best if they were things you could most easily do without?

Actually packing the car requires only 15 minutes or so, particularly if you prepare for it well. You could have a trial packing session, but if you apply common sense in planning and preparing, you probably won't need a practice session. When you do pack the small car, there's something satisfying about making everything fit into place. You see your judgment pay off, and that helps put you in a good frame of mind to begin a long drive.

Notice that the author of this theme included a paragraph to discuss equipment. The major piece of equipment needed if you are to pack a small car is obvious enough, of course, but the author used the extra paragraph to discuss the necessity of assessing whether the small car by itself is sufficient for the task. At the same time, however, the author did not wander off into a lengthy discussion of the ways of expanding the carrying space; mentioning the options was pertinent, but lengthy discussion of them would have destroyed the unity of the theme. Notice also that each step in the packing process is clearly identified, with helpful suggestions and possible pitfalls clearly explained. Throughout the paper, transitions connect the steps with words like *first, second,* and *finally.* These kinds of transitions are especially important in a process description.

VARYING FROM THE MODEL THEME

This paper varies from the model five-paragraph essay in several small ways: it has six paragraphs; not all paragraphs have standard topic sentences; and the conclusion does not present a reworded thesis statement. The skeleton of a five-paragraph essay gives the basic form to the paper, of course, but the equipment paragraph after the introduction increases the paragraph count to six. Also the topic sentence for paragraph three merely identifies the step of the process, without giving any reminder of the thesis, and the topic sentence for paragraph four, which also identifies the step, is the second sentence in that paragraph. Finally, although the conclusion clearly deals with the connection between common sense and the preparatory steps in the packing process, there is no simple rewording of the thesis statement; instead, the repetition of the thesis idea is placed in the context of rejecting the need for a practice packing session.

EXERCISES

A. From the list of topics below, select three that interest you. Use the example as a guide and narrow the topics as indicated; then divide the narrowed topic into major steps.

TOPICS

Cleaning	Driving	Literary Characters
Firemaking	Hobbies	Gardening
Maturing	Remodeling	Jobs
	Famous Battles	

   1. (Example) Topic: Cleaning
                      Limited Topic: Loading a dishwasher

                    Steps: 1. Scraping and rinsing

                                  2. Loading china

     3.   Loading glassware _____

     4.   Loading silverware _____

2.   Topic:
    Limited Topic:

    Steps: _____

           _____

           _____

           _____

           _____

3.   Topic:
    Limited Topic:

    Steps: _____

           _____

           _____

           _____

           _____

           _____

4.   Topic:
    Limited topic:

    Steps: _____

           _____

           _____

           _____

           _____

           _____

B.   Select the narrowed topic that interests you and write a paragraph that covers the *second* step. Be sure to use the transitions you need to signal your reader.

C.   Select a broad subject, narrow it, and write a process description. Topics in Exercise A might suggest a place to begin. If you vary from the model of the five-paragraph essay, list your variations on a separate page at the end of the paper. If you borrow material from another source, be sure to document it.

PART V

THE RESEARCH PAPER

You've probably been having nightmares about the research paper ever since we first mentioned it. Actually, you already know most of the skills involved. You know the fundamentals of organization and support, and you've probably studied the punctuation and expression chapters. You've even used some outside sources and a simple method of documentation. The only new skills you need to learn are efficient ways to find your support in the library, organize it, use it in the paper, and document it. You'll find these new skills demand more time and patience than you needed for your earlier papers, but they are not difficult to learn.

CHAPTER 17

Overview of the Research Paper

Sooner or later the longer paper comes to us all, usually because it's assigned or perhaps because we find ourselves interested in a subject. But regardless of the reason, we're all faced with the same problem. How do we say anything intelligent for five or ten pages or more?

Either we write about a subject we know intimately, or we go to some other source—an interview with an eyewitness, perhaps, or a book in the library. When we must use sources outside our own minds or experience, we rely on research.

Unlike some of the earlier exercises and paragraphs in this book, the research paper has *no invented evidence.* You must find the specific support for your research paper by consulting real sources, not imaginary ones.

By now you may be worried because of stories you've heard about research papers. A research paper can be long and it can be a lot of work, especially if you put it off until the day before it's due. But you may also have heard some wrong statements about the long paper; let's get rid of those ideas now.

WHAT IT'S NOT

The research paper is not
   —a rehash of encyclopedia articles
   —a string of quotations one after the other like sausages
   —a mass of invented support
   —a mystical kind of writing that is more difficult than the kind you
      have been doing.

WHAT IT IS

The research paper is
- —an organized statement about a subject, using support from sources outside your experience
- —one that credits sources with notes and a bibliography
- —a normal requirement in many college courses and professional jobs
- —the next step in your development as a writer.

This chapter and the ones to follow will help you take that step. They will show you what a research paper looks like, how to organize it, how to present your research in a paper, and how to give credit for ideas and words you borrow.

THE SHAPE OF THE RESEARCH PAPER

Like the writing you did earlier, the research paper is an expanded form of the five-paragraph essay. Of course it's longer, but the basic structure is still the same. Let's look at the relationship between a five-paragraph essay and a longer research paper. Study the chart on the next page.

Not every paragraph must have exactly three items of specific support, nor must every main idea have exactly three paragraphs of support. Some may have more, some less. Whatever the number, the support paragraphs help persuade your readers to accept one of the major topic sentences in the same way specific support helps persuade them to accept the topic sentences in a five-paragraph essay. And the major topic sentences in the research paper help convince your readers of the thesis. By now you've learned that a model is simply a guide, a handy way to begin thinking about your paper. Treat this model the same way.

RESEARCH PAPER: PURPOSE AND PROCESS

But, you may ask, now that we know the basic shape of a research paper, what is a research paper anyway? The basic purpose of a longer paper could be to explore a particular problem (the major cause of the British defeat at Singapore, for example), or to inform your readers of a development (the effects of an increase in the minimum wage), or to trace the history of a particular situation (how America became involved in the Panama Canal). Keep in mind that the research paper is not just a classroom exercise; it has many practical uses, too. Businesses use research papers as marketing studies or as reports to stockholders; the military

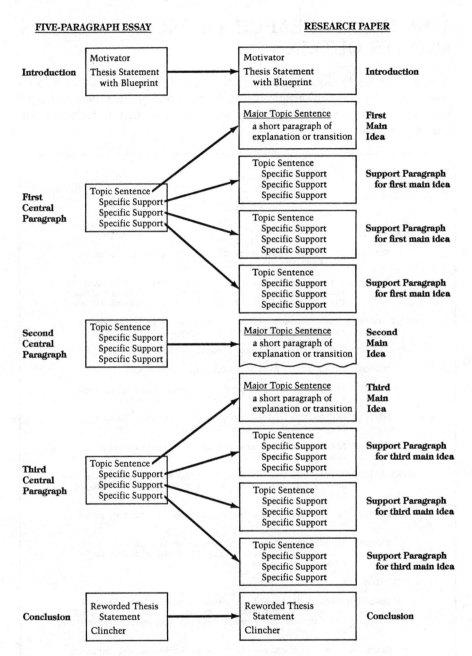

FIVE-PARAGRAPH ESSAY   RESEARCH PAPER

services call them staff studies; doctors call them case studies; professors sometimes call them monographs.

Regardless of the term we use, the important thing to note is that the *process* is the same: study the problem, gather the facts, assemble the facts, write a draft, revise it, and prepare the final version.

A SAMPLE RESEARCH PAPER
AND ITS OUTLINE

To see what can be done in about five manuscript pages or about a thousand words, look at the sample research paper one of our students wrote. To help you see the skeleton of organization we've also included an outline of the paper.

<u>Outline</u>

INTRODUCTION

    Motivator: Most people know little about French help in the Revolutionary War.

    Thesis Statement with Blueprint: The physical presence of skilled officers, troops, and naval fleets enabled the Thirteen Colonies to become the United States.

FIRST MAJOR TOPIC: French officers skilled in engineering or field leadership were indispensable.

    SUPPORT PARAGRAPH: Engineers contributed.

    SUPPORT PARAGRAPH: Field leadership was important.

SECOND MAJOR TOPIC: Thousands of French troops provided enough force to allow the Allied forces to win.

    SUPPORT PARAGRAPH: Early battles with French aid were unsuccessful but significant.

    SUPPORT PARAGRAPH: The army at the Yorktown victory was more than half French.

THIRD MAJOR TOPIC: The French navy, nearly all of America's sea power, had a significant effect on the outcome of the war.

    SUPPORT PARAGRAPH: Early naval battles diverted English sea forces.

    SUPPORT PARAGRAPH: French sea power at the battle of Chesapeake Bay led to the ultimate victory at Yorktown.

CONCLUSION

    Reworded Thesis Statement: French generals and admirals helped plan the battle, French engineers prepared the battle, and French sailors and soldiers fought in the battle.

    Clincher: Without this aid, both at Yorktown and earlier, it is improbable that the Americans could have defeated the British and won independence.

James E. Kinzer
English 111 H
Professor Whitlock
April 20, 1979

The Effects of French Military Aid

on the American Revolutionary War

While almost all Americans know that the French helped
the American cause during the Revolutionary War, few know any
more than that the Marquis de Lafayette was a general in the
Continental Army. Yet, French aid to the Colonies was as ex-
tensive as it was varied, ranging from arms and troops to mon-
etary gifts and loans. The French gave the Americans millions
of pounds in specie, and more than half the Army's weaponry
was French after 1776.[1] However, even though the French aid
to the Colonies was diverse, the physical presence of skilled
officers, troops, and naval fleets enabled the Thirteen Colonies to become the United States.

Although formal French assistance to the Americans began
shortly after the signing of the French-American Alliance on
February 6, 1778, many French officers, skilled in engineering
or battlefield leadership, came to America prior to that time
to offer their support. Indeed, one historian says of the foreign officers, "Some were indispensable, and perhaps there could
not have been a competent, balanced American army without them.
This is especially true of specialized branches like the engineers, cavalry and staff."[2]

Among the specialized branches, perhaps the engineers'
help was the most important. The group of French engineers
was led by Louis Le Begue Duportail, who arrived early in
1777. These officers provided vital skills and direction to
an army that had no one trained in the important science of
military engineering. One key task Duportail accomplished
was building barracks, batteries, and fortifications at West
Point in the fall of 1779.[3] Duportail, commissioned a brigadier
general by Congress, became an important advisor to General
Washington. Washington depended heavily on Duportail and Colonel Gouvion, another French engineer, for technical information and advice.[4] A final area in which the engineers played
a major role was the design of the siege of Yorktown. There,
the French experts planned and supervised the building of
trenches and redoubts, troop assembly depots, and fortifications that were crucial to the success of the land operations.[5]

Other French officers provided organizational and leadership skills, which were lacking in the Continental Army.
The young Marquis de Lafayette is the most notable example,
but many others led armies and navies in successful campaigns.
The Comte de Rochambeau, a major general, helped Washington
in planning for Yorktown and led a French division there.
Colonel Armand (Marquis de La Rouerie), although not successful,
led a cavalry brigade at Camden, South Carolina, in August
1780.[6] Admiral Comte d'Estaing captured several West Indies
islands and participated in two combined land-sea operations.[7]

3

Admiral Comte de Grasse, who chose the site of battle for the decisive Yorktown campaign in 1781, outmaneuvered and defeated Admiral Graves in the Chesapeake Bay.[8] Thus, experienced French officers provided much of the necessary leadership for the American army.

However, it takes more than just officers to win a war; the French sent over thousands of troops who provided the Americans sufficient force to win battles. French troops and ships first arrived on American shores on July 7, 1778, under the command of the Comte Charles d'Estaing. According to William B. Wilcox, editor of Sir Henry Clinton's The American Rebellion, the entry of France "transformed the whole character of the war."[9] Although early land engagements were largely unsuccessful for the French and American forces, the French presence caused the British to change their strategy.

One of the earliest battles occurred when Comte d'Estaing, anxious to engage the enemy, sailed into Narragansett Bay, Rhode Island, in late July for a joint land-sea siege of Newport with forces under General Sullivan. D'Estaing managed to capture only three British ships before he was forced by weather to withdraw, but his presence caused Britain to divert some of its forces and to abandon Philadelphia.[10] In the South, meanwhile, Colonel Armand and his cavalry brigade participated in the attack on Camden. Although he was equally unsuccessful, his brigade greatly augmented General Gates' forces and enabled the battle to occur in the first place.[11] D'Estaing made another attempt at a siege in September 1779. This time he and General Benjamin

4

Lincoln laid seige to Savannah, Georgia. The allied forces,
about 3500 French soldiers and 1000 Americans, attacked on
October 9, but were repulsed because delays in setting up the
attack gave the defenders time to prepare for it.[12] This
apparent failure, too, had positive effects; according to historian Stanley Idzerda, the battle of Savannah "helped convince
the British commander . . . that he should move his main operations to the South" to defend against such attacks.[13] Thus,
the early battles, although tactically unsuccessful, were
strategically important because, as historian William Stinchcombe
says, "the mere presence of the French Army and Fleet significantly altered British miltary planning."[14]

Not until the battle of Yorktown in October 1781, however,
did the French allies successfully engage the British. Five
separate armies, two of them French, converged on Virginia in
September. Of the total of 15,000 Allied troops at Yorktown,
nearly 8000 were French. These French armies, one of 4000 led
by the Comte de Rochambeau and the other of 3700 led by the
Comte de Saint-Simon, led the assault on the town of York from
the western half.[15] The American victory at Yorktown, then, was
actually accomplished by a force that was more than one-half
French.

While the French armies significantly aided the Continental
Army, the French navy constituted nearly all of America's sea
power and was probably the biggest factor in the victory of the
Colonies. The importance was that England no longer ruled the
sea uncontested and that she had lost the advantage of mobility

by losing control of the sea.[16]

The French navy, though not always victorious at first,
caused a major shift in British sea strategy. The Comte
d'Estaing, as previously mentioned, was not tactically victorious,
but provided the Americans with a moral victory by his presence.
In addition, he managed to capture two British-held islands in
the West Indies in early 1781, forcing the British to augment
their naval forces there by diverting ships from Admiral Howe's
fleet.[17] At approximately the same time, Admiral Destouches in
Newport engaged Admiral Arbuthnot and managed to keep the port
there in Allied hands.[18]

The French navy met with far greater success at the battle
of Chesapeake Bay, off Yorktown. The main French fleet present
was that of Admiral Francois Joseph Paul de Grasse. Admiral
de Grasse sailed up from the Caribbean Sea for six weeks to
assist the Americans before he had to return to assist the
Spanish. He arrived in Chesapeake Bay on August 30, 1781,
with a fleet of twenty-nine ships and 3700 troops, blocking
off Lord Cornwallis' sea escape.[19] When the British fleet of
twenty-four ships under the command of Admiral Graves and
Admirals Drake and Hood arrived September 5, it found the
bay blocked. The ensuing battle was a standoff, but de Grasse
managed to maintain the blockade. By September 10, Admiral
de Barras had arrived from Newport with seven ships. This
additional force made the tally thirty-six to twenty-four against
the British, and Admiral Graves retreated to New York in the face
of these odds.[20] Admiral de Grasse's fleet had prevented

6

Cornwallis' escape; hence, one can understand why a historian
would suggest that "sea power had been decisive in making the
surrender of Cornwallis to the Allied armies virtually inevitable."[21]
Certainly the outcome of the battle, and perhaps the war, would
have been different had the British had uncontested control of
the sea.

The French, then, provided many technicians and leaders,
thousands of troops, and dozens of ships to the Colonies during
the Revolutionary War. Especially at Yorktown, the major Allied
victory, the dependence on France was evident. French generals
and admirals helped plan the battle; French engineers prepared
the battle; and French sailors and soldiers fought in the battle.
Without this aid, both at Yorktown and earlier, it is improbable
that the Americans could have defeated the British and won
independence.

Notes

[1]Maurice Matloff, ed., American Military History
(Washington, D.C.: Office of the Chief of Military History,
1969), p. 99.

[2]Aram Bakshian, "Foreign Adventurers in the American
Revolution," History Today, 21 (March 1971), 187.

[3]Elizabeth S. Kite, Brigadier-General Louis Le Bègue
Duportail (Baltimore: The Johns Hopkins Press, 1933), p. 145.

[4]Kite, p. 165.

[5]The French Army, Corps of Engineers, French Engineers
and the American War of Independence, trans. Sylvia G. Goldfrank
(New York: French Embassy Information Service, 1975), p. 12.

[6]Bakshian, p. 189.

[7]Stanley J. Idzerda, ed., France and the American War for
Independence (n.p.: Scott Limited Editions, Inc., n.d.),
pp. 37-39.

[8]Idzerda, pp. 43-44.

[9]William B. Wilcox, ed., Introd., The American Rebellion,
by Sir Henry Clinton (New Haven: Yale University Press, 1954),
p. xxix.

[10]Matloff, p. 89.

[11]Bakshian, p. 194.

[12]Rupert Furneaux, The Pictorial History of the American
Revolution (Chicago: J.G. Ferguson, 1973), p. 295.

[13]Idzerda, p. 39.

[14]William C. Stinchcombe, The American Revolution and
the French Alliance (Syracuse, N.Y.: Syracuse University Press,
1969), p. 152.

[15]Stephan Bonsal, When the French Were Here (Port Washington,
N.Y.: Kennikat Press, 1945), p. 139.

[16]Dave Palmer, "American Strategy Reconsidered," as quoted
in Stanley J. Underdal, ed., Military History of the American
Revolution (Washington, D.C.: Office of Air Force History,
Headquarters USAF, 1976), p. 59.

8

[17]Willard M. Wallace, Appeal to Arms (New York: Harper & Row, 1951), p. 230.

[18]Arnold Whitridge, "Rochambeau and the American Revolution," History Today, 12 (May 1962), 317.

[19]Furneaux, p. 295.

[20]Jack Coggins, Ships and Seamen of the American Revolution (Harrisburg, Pa.: Stackpole Books, 1969), p. 201.

[21]Wallace, p. 255.

9

Selected Bibliography

Bakshian, Aram. "Foreign Adventurers in the American Revolution."
    History Today, 21 (March 1971), 187-97.

Bonsal, Stephan. When the French Were Here. Port Washington,
    N.Y.: Kennikat Press, 1945.

Coggins, Jack. Ships and Seamen of the American Revolution.
    Harrisburg, Pa.: Stackpole Books, 1969.

The French Army, Corps of Engineers. French Engineers and
    the American War of Independence. Trans. Sylvia G. Gold-
    frank. New York: French Embassy Information Service, 1975.

Furneaux, Rupert. The Pictorial History of the American Rev-
    olution. Chicago: J.G. Ferguson, 1973.

Idzerda, Stanley J., ed. France and the American War for Inde-
    pendence. n.p.: Scott Limited Editions, Inc., n.d.

Kite, Elizabeth S. Brigadier-General Louis Le Bègue Duportail.
    Baltimore: The Johns Hopkins Press, 1933.

Matloff, Maurice, ed. American Military History. Washington,
    D.C.: Office of the Chief of Military History, 1969.

Stinchcombe, William C. The American Revolution and the French
    Alliance. Syracuse, N.Y.: Syracuse University Press, 1969.

Underdal, Stanley J., ed. Military History of the American Rev-
    olution. Washington, D.C.: Office of Air Force History,
    Headquarters USAF, 1976.

Wallace, Willard M. Appeal to Arms. New York: Harper & Row,
    1951.

10

Whitridge, Arnold. "Rochambeau and the American Revolution."
    History Today, 12 (May 1962), 312-20.

Wilcox, William B., ed., introd. The American Rebellion. By
    Sir Henry Clinton. New Haven: Yale University Press, 1954.

CHAPTER 18

Finding Support

Let's be honest about it. Many times when you have to write a research paper you won't know much about the subject, so you won't know what you want to say until you've studied the subject enough to narrow it to something manageable, to a thesis. For example, from the broad subject of "welfare" you might narrow to "welfare cheaters" and even further to the narrow thesis that "welfare cheaters are a majority of those on welfare."

WHERE TO BEGIN

One way both to narrow your topic and to get a lead on the information is to do some preliminary research in general reference tools, such as encyclopedias. At this point, begin to keep an informal record of your research by listing briefly the title and the headings or subjects you looked under. This step is especially important if you later want to return to pick up that bit of information you remember reading but didn't write down.

As you continue in your research, you may well be in for some surprises, for what you find may take you in new directions. Despite your earlier belief, for example, you might find that welfare chiselers are really few in number and that needy people are not crooks. When such a change happens, you must revise your thesis; in this case, you might say something like "Despite popular opinion to the contrary, welfare cheaters are a minority of those on welfare."

Once you have a thesis, you are ready to begin the more formal research process. The problem is to know where to begin to find the best written support for your subject. You may begin with either books or periodicals. Let's say you decide to start with books.

The primary guide to a library's book collection is normally the card catalog. Cards come in three kinds: author, subject, and title. If you know the author of a book you want, look under his or her name. If you know the title, you can look there. But sometimes you know only a general subject, say Shakespeare criticism. Then you can look at cards under that heading.

In any case, the information on the cards will save you time. If you were working on a paper about Shakespeare's tragedies, you might come across an author card such as the one on this page.

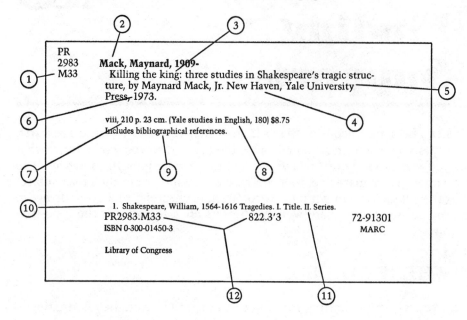

1. call number, to help you find the book on the library shelf
2. author's name
3. title
4. place of publication
5. publisher
6. publication date (choose the most recent edition when you can)
7. number of pages
8. this book is part of a series
9. note on special content (a bibliography is especially important, for it can lead you to other related books)
10. subject heading where another card for this book is filed and where you might find other books
11. notation that other cards for this book are filed under title and series
12. recommended Library of Congress and Dewey decimal system call numbers

Title and subject cards look just like author cards except that the book title or reference subject is typed on top so the cards can be alphabetized more easily by title or subject. Often all three types of cards are filed together alphabetically, but the card types may be filed separately, depending on the library.

Here's how you might use the card catalog. Let's say you saw a television special on "The Rise and Fall of the Third Reich" and you became interested in Hitler's follower, Hermann Göring, commander of the German Air Force (the Luftwaffe). You would obviously look under his name and probably under *Germany, Luftwaffe* where you find some more titles. The leads suggested by the subject headings would soon bring you to Hitler, Heinkel, Fokker, and Goebbels. Eventually you'd come to such subjects as *World War, 1939–1945—Aerial operations* and perhaps to *War Crime Trials—Nuremberg, 1945–6*. This process has helped you identify essential books on the subject.

As you consult the card catalog, be sure to jot down the exact call number, author's name, and brief title of the book. This information helps you find the book on the shelf or gives you the basic data for requesting a recall of the book if it's out of the library (and if your library recalls books).

PERIODICALS

The card catalog, however, isn't the only way to find support you need for your research. Periodicals, which include popular magazines and professional journals, are also basic sources—and you should remember that even the most recent book is at least a year out of date by the time it appears, and the information in it may be several years old. As a result, if your topic requires last-minute, up-to-date information, you may need to use some periodicals.

How do you find what you need? You could, of course, go to the library stacks and start leafing through all the bound volumes of *U.S. News and World Report* in hope you'd find the article you need. But even just looking at the table of contents in each issue would take more time than you can afford. So what do you do? Find a shortcut to get to the information quickly. That's where reference tools come in. They help you find the right article, as the card catalog helped you find the right book. The problem is that there is more than one "card catalog" for periodicals.

Let's say, for example, that you want to write about American Indians. That's too big a topic, so you narrow it to the problems of modern American Indians, which is still pretty broad. You go further to decide on the thesis that land and resource claims of modern American Indians are once again bringing the Indians into conflict with their neighbors and with themselves. After checking the card catalog for books, you decide to try your hand at periodicals. You check one of the most widely known indexes, the *Readers' Guide to Periodical Literature*, because you remember it from high school. On page 231 of the issue covering April 22 to July 21, 1981, under the major heading of *INDIANS of North America*, you find these subheadings with entries:

Land tenure

Growing sense of northern déjà vu [reactivation of Indian
land claims issue as National Energy Board gives go-ahead
to oil pipeline in Mackenzie Valley, Northwest Terri-
tories] G. Legge. il map Macleans 94:40+ My 4 '81
This land is whose land [Canada; with editorial comment by
P. C. Newman] R. MacGregor. il pors map Macleans 94:3,
49+ Je 1 '81

Land utilization

Indian harvest white man style [land tenure controversy involving use of Sarcee land for housing development for
non-Indian residents in Alberta] G. Legge. il Macleans
94:36 Je 15 '81

Mines and mineral resources

Navajo mineral swindle: wheeling and dealing on the reservation [Interior Department vs lawyer N. Littell] M.
Miller and others. por USA Today 109:56–60 My '81*

What good are these entries? Well, they tell us that people named
Legge and MacGregor wrote articles about Indian land claims in Canada
and that someone named Miller, who had coauthors, wrote about a mineral controversy on the Navajo reservation. Note that each title entry
gives a volume or issue number, followed after the colon by the page
number and the abbreviated date. Notice also that commentary in
brackets expands on the article's content when the title isn't self-explanatory. Of course, we really can't be sure whether the articles will help
until we read them.

We ought to add a caution here. The *Readers' Guide* covers about
160 magazines and journals that are considered to contain articles of general (or "popular" interest): *Reader's Digest, Time, U.S. News and World
Report, Cosmopolitan, Popular Mechanics,* and the like. Since it doesn't
cover professional or scholarly journals, it may not help much for scholarly topics, but it's worth checking if you are working on a topic that
would be covered by general-interest magazines.

Don't stop here. Try another index. The *Public Affairs Information
Service Bulletin* (or *PAIS*) is like the *Readers' Guide,* but it may be more
helpful because it covers 1400 periodicals, as well as some books and government documents. Here's a portion of the articles under the major
heading *INDIANS* from page 489 of the *PAIS* for October 1980–September 1981:

Land ownership

Christie, John C., jr. Indian claims and the land title
industry. *Title News* 59:7–11+ D '80

† Kammer, Jerry. The second long walk: the Navajo-Hopi
land dispute [Arizona]. '80 xvii + 239p il maps index
(LC 80–52273) (ISBN 0-8263-0549-0) $14.95—*Univ N
Mex Pr*

† United States. House. Com. on the Judiciary. Subcom.
on Admin. Law and Governmental Relations. Statute
of limitations for certain claims by the United States
on behalf of Indians: hearing, February 27, 1980, on S.
2222, to extend the time for commencing actions on
behalf of an Indian tribe, band, or group, or on behalf
of an individual Indian whose land is held in trust or
restricted status. '80 iii+ 61p chart (96th Cong., 2d
Sess.) (Serial no. 40) pa—*Washington, DC 20515*

† United States. Senate. Select Com. on Indian Affairs.
Proposed settlement of Maine Indian land claims:
hearings, July 1–2, 1980, on S. 2829. '80 2v (1344p)
bibl il tables charts maps (96th Cong., 2d Sess.)
pa—*Washington, DC 20510*

Legal status, laws, etc.

Burness, H. S. and others. United States reclamation
policy and Indian water rights. tables *Natural
Resources J 20:807–26 O '80*

Griffith, Gwendolyn. Indian claims to groundwater:
reserved rights or beneficial interest? *Stanford Law R
33:103–30 N '80**

The format of the entries is similar to that in the *Readers' Guide.* Again there's a brief summary of the article if the title isn't self-explanatory. Notice the three entries marked with dagger symbols; those entries are for a book and two U.S. government publications. You may be looking for periodical articles, but don't pass up this valuable information in the meantime.

As useful as they are, these indexes cover a total of only about two percent of the published articles. Another kind of reference tool, an abstract, may help even more. There are thousands of abstracts, covering hundreds of topics. You must consult the specialized index for abstracts for your subject. An abstract summarizes the contents of a technical or scholarly article, but the abstract is longer than the brief summary in the *PAIS.*

For example, if you want to find out about the effect of electrical power plants on the environment, you might look at an abstract. Here's one from *GEO Abstracts C (Economic Geography)* for 1977/1, under the category *Environmental Economics:*

77C/0088 Legal and regulatory issues in air quality management for the Electric Power Industry. HAL B.H. COOPER Jr & TROY B. WEBB, Journal Air Pollution Control Association, 26(7), 1976, pp 647–649.
A Conference on Air Quality Management in the Electric Power Industry was held at The University of Texas at Austin in Austin, TX, on January 28–30, 1976. The opening session of the Conference was devoted to legal and regulatory issues in air pollution control related to the electric power industry. The purpose of this session was to present the viewpoints of those Federal and state regulatory agencies most directly involved in air pollution control for the electric power industry. Emphasis was placed on those issues relating to the increasing need for coal and oil

---

combustion to meet the Nation's electrical energy requirements, concentrating on the five southwestern states of Arkansas, Louisiana, New Mexico, Oklahoma, and Texas in Federal Region VI.   –Authors*

Remember, this is not the article but a summary. So what can you use here? First, the abstract is useful as an indicator of the content of the article it summarizes. But it's like a metal detector. It can only tell you it's there, not how valuable it is. To use the article, you must read it. Second, the abstract number can make it easier if you have time for the librarian to order a copy of the original. As a general rule, don't cite abstracts in your footnotes or bibliography. Go to the original.

What happens if you've been to all these sources and still haven't found what you want? Don't give up, for this is where the challenge of research comes in. Your library will have many more research tools to help you get the paper written.

Among the more common reference tools besides those we've already mentioned, you might find these in your library:

> *Annual Bibliography of English Language and Literature:* indexes articles and books about authors and literature written in English.
> *Art Index:* art periodicals, both professional and scholarly.
> *Biography Index:* an index to biographical material on living and historical figures.
> *Biological Abstracts:* abstracts covering articles on biosciences published in professional journals worldwide.
> *Book Review Digest:* summary of book reviews for modern literature; useful for finding out how a book was received.
> *Business Periodicals Index:* as title indicates, index of business and economic articles.
> *Chemical Abstracts:* abstracts of research articles in chemistry.
> *Education Index:* for articles dealing with education research and development.
> *Essay and General Literature Index:* author and subject index to collections of essays.
> *MLA International Bibliography:* published annually by the Modern Language Association; covers scholarly journals and books about language and literature in English and other modern languages.
> *New York Times Index:* a key, comprehensive index to all news events in *The New York Times*; a basic tool, good for almost any topic.
> *Social Sciences, Humanities, and General Sciences Indexes:* a fam-

---

* Reproduced from Geo Abstracts C, 1977/1, by permission of Geo Abstracts Ltd. and the Air Pollution Control Association.

ily of indexes covering scholarly and professional journals on these subjects. (The *International Index,* published 1907–65, became the *Social Sciences and Humanities Index,* which split in 1974 into the *Social Sciences Index* and the *Humanities Index;* the *General Sciences Index* joined the family in 1978.)

Other good sources of help are subject bibliographies. They list all the books and articles on a limited subject, such as G. B. Shaw, novels in the nineteenth century, or the Battle of Gettysburg. Consult an experienced librarian for help in finding a bibliography in your subject.

Finally, talk to a reference librarian for more ideas. One of your goals, however, should be to become self-sufficient in your library research so that you can move quickly and surely to solve the problems for yourself. To help you begin, we have prepared the following exercises.

EXERCISES

A. Use the index cards on the next page to answer questions 1 through 7.

    1. This card (and its continuation) is an example of
      a. a subject card
      b. a title card
      c. an author card
      d. an alpha-designator card

    2. What is the Library of Congress call number? _____
    3. How many pages are in the book, including introductory material? _____
    4. Who is the publisher? _____

    5. What is the date of publication? _____
    6. Can we tell from the card authors of specific essays? _____
    7. Use the cross-references on this card to find a card on one of the subjects. List the author, title, place of publication, publisher, date, and your library's call number. _____

B. Answer one of the following exercises as your instructor directs.

    1. On April 2, 1972, Sen. Edward Kennedy introduced to Congress a bill to preserve the natural beauty of Nantucket Island, Mass., by regulating land development. If you wanted to find out what was written about that bill, you might use the *Public Affairs Information Service (PAIS).* If so, you would search for published information beginning with what *PAIS* volume?

PS
3555   **Ellison, Ralph.   Invisible Man**
.L625   Trimmer, Joseph F   comp.
I538   A casebook on Ralph Ellison's Invisible man. Edited by
        Joseph F. Trimmer. New York, T. Y. Crowell [1972]

        viii, 321 p. 21 cm.

        CONTENTS: Atlanta Exposition address, by B. T. Washington.—Of Mr.
        Booker T. Washington and others, by W. E. B. DuBois.—The new Negro, by
        A. Locke.—An appeal to the conscience of the Black race to see itself, by M.
        Garvey.—I tried to be a Communist, by R. Wright.—The poet, by R. W.
        Emerson.—Tradition and the individual talent, by T. S. Eliot.—Negro
        character as seen by white authors, by S. A. Brown.—Black boys and native
        sons, by I. Howe.—The world and the jug, by R. Ellison.—Ralph Ellison and
        the uses of imagination, by R. Bone.—Ralph Ellison and the birth of the
        anti-hero, by W. J. Schafer.

                            (Continued on next card)

                                                            75-179779
                              72   MARC

PS
3555   **Ellison, Ralph. Invisible Man**
.L625   Trimmer, Joseph F   comp. A casebook on Ralph Ellison's
I538   Invisible man . . . [1972] (Card 2)
                            CONTENTS—Continued.

        —The rebirth of the artist, by E. Horowitz.—Ralph Ellison and the American
        comic tradition, by E. H. Rovit.—Sight imagery in Invisible man, by A.
        Bloch.—Whitman and Ellison: older symbols in a modern mainstream, by
        M. E. Mengeling.—Ralph Ellison's modern version of Brer Bear and Brer
        Rabbit in Invisible man, by F. R. Horowitz:—The politics of Ellison's Booker:
        Invisible man as symbolic history, by R. Kostelanetz.—Brave words for a
        startling occasion, by R. Ellison.—Bibliography (p. 311–316)

        1. Ellison, Ralph. Invisible man. 2. Negroes—History. I. Title.
        PS3555.L625I538   813'.5'4   75-179779
        ISBN 0-690-17921-9   MARC

        Library of Congress   72

a.   Volume number _____

b.   What subject entry or entries would you use to search for
published information on the bill? _____
_____

c.   In *PAIS* Vol. 59, page 576, you find an article covering the
Kennedy bill. Answer the following questions:

    (1) What is the title of the article? _____

_____

    (2) Who is the author? _____

    (3) Who published the article and when? _____

_____

    (4) What is the volume number for the published work? _____

    (5) On what page does the article begin? _____

2. On December 3, 1970, the U.S. Senate voted against additional spending to develop a supersonic transport (SST). Research an editorial *The New York Times* published "lauding the Senate vote against further government spending for development of a supersonic airliner."

  a. On what date did the editorial appear? _____

  b. On what page? _____
  c. What reference tool did you use to find the information? _____

_____

3. In 1965, Cloyte M. Larsson wrote a book for the Johnson Publishing Co. dealing with interracial marriage. The book can be found listed in what volume of the *Public Affairs Information Service (PAIS)*?

  a. Volume _____   Page _____
  b. What subjects might you research in *PAIS* to find this article?

    (1) _____

    (2) _____

    (3) _____

    (4) _____
  c. The book reprinted articles from what magazines?

    (1) _____

    (2) _____

    (3) _____

4. In July 1974 a periodical carried an article on the views of R.

Heinlein, who is a science-fiction author. Using the *Readers' Guide to Periodical Literature,* locate the following:

    a. What periodical carried the article?

        (1) Title _____

        (2) Volume _____

        (3) Date _____   Page _____

Find the article in the work listed and answer the following:

    b. What college did Heinlein attend? _____

CHAPTER 19

Taking and Organizing Notes

Let's review for a moment. You settle on a general topic and narrow it as much as you reasonably can. Your preliminary reading helps you focus the topic and at the same time reassures you that sources appear to be available for you to draw on for support material. For example, let's say you're interested in those prehistoric people who left their homes on the Asian continent and for some reason found their way to the American continent and developed new lives here. You realize that "prehistoric Indians" is too large a topic, so you reduce it to "prehistoric Indians in North America," to the new way of life in America. That, you decide, still is too broad, but it's a place to start with your preliminary reading. This preliminary exploration of the topic leads you to a new, interesting idea: contrary to the popular belief you've heard for years that the prehistoric Indians wandered across the American continent struggling to survive, there is relatively recent evidence that the prehistoric Indians adapted well and produced sophisticated cultures. Your preliminary reading also suggests that your library holds enough sources to support your research, so you use the card catalog and the indexes and bibliographies of your library's reference section to make a list of books and periodical articles that look promising. Now what? Here's where the work begins.

You obviously can't remember every idea or fact you find in your reading. You could keep all the books and magazines piled up around you and then flip through them to find a bit of support when you needed it. But that's the hard way. The easiest, most time-saving way to gather support is to take careful notes on what you might use.

WHAT TO DO: BIBLIOGRAPHY CARDS

Pick the most likely looking book and check the table of contents or index to see which parts of the book apply. (It's just not sensible to read the entire book if only Chapter 2 deals with prehistoric American Indians.)

If the book has nothing useful, put it aside to return to the library as soon as you can. Someone else may need it.

When you find a book that has information you think you might use, make out a *bibliography card*. If your instructor has no preference, use either 3" × 5" index cards or slips. This size is convenient enough to put in your pocket but has enough space for all the information you need.

Record only one book on each slip and be careful to include all the data about the book. For *books*, you'll need all of the following items later (the ones that apply) when you're preparing your notes and bibliography pages for your final paper: author(s) or group responsible; title and subtitle (and volume title if part of a multivolume set); translator(s); editor(s); edition (don't worry about the number of "printings," but do note the edition if the book is other than the first edition); volume number(s); place of publication (the first one listed if there are several); publisher; date of publication (latest copyright date, not the date of printing). You can save yourself time later by putting all the items in the correct bibliographic format (Chapters 21 and 22 will explain note and bibliography entries). However, don't worry at this point about getting the format right if you don't know it. Here's a sample working bibliography card—it has all the needed information, but we've not concerned ourselves with bibliographic form.

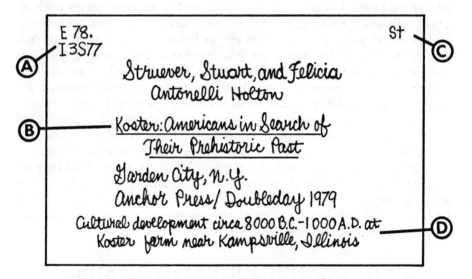

Note these things about the working bibliography card:

A.   Always include the *library call number*; it will save you time if you have to go back to recheck a quotation or find information you forgot to copy down.

B.   Include all the applicable information (author, title, publisher, etc.) from the list above.

C.　Add your own *bibliography code.* We use the first two letters of the first author's last name. But you may use any consistent system —numbering, small letters, Roman numerals. The coding system will save you time as you take notes and as you write drafts of your paper.

D.　*Optional.* As a reminder, add a brief note about what the book contains.

With your first working bibliography card, you've begun to compile your paper's working bibliography. As you consult the books and articles you've found, prepare a separate card for each one. For *articles in periodicals* (magazines, journals, and newspapers), you'll need some or all of the following information (as applicable) on your working bibliography cards: author(s) (articles may be unsigned, and sometimes you'll find only initials for the author); title of article; type of article (e.g., letters to the editor and reviews); name of periodical; series number (such as "old" or "new"); newspaper edition (if the newspaper publishes more than one edition per day); volume and/or issue number; date of publication; inclusive page numbers for the article. Also note whether the periodical is paginated continuously throughout a volume or independently issue by issue. For example, if issue 2 of a volume ends with page 563 and issue 3 of the same volume begins with page 564, the publication paginates issues continuously throughout a volume. If each issue starts with page 1, then the issues are paginated separately. This distinction won't matter for your research, but it will help you decide which format to use when you write your note and bibliographic entries for the final paper. (Again, Chapters 21 and 22 explain note and bibliographic forms.)

WHAT TO DO: NOTE CARDS

When you come across a fact or idea you think you can use, make a *note card.* Again, use 3" × 5" cards or slips. *Important:* put only one fact or idea on each card. When you are ready to use the information for your draft, you will be much freer to move the cards if you have only one idea on each card.

Now read the following passage from page 244 of the Struever and Holton book about the archaeological diggings at the Koster farm near Kampsville, Illinois. ("Horizon 11" is the designation for a level of human occupation dating to about 6400 B.C.)

> Traditionally, archaeologists have assumed that Archaic people went through a long, slow, gradual process in learning how to cope with their environment and how to extract a decent living from it.

They thought it took the aborigines several thousand years, from Paleo-Indian times (circa 12,000–8000 B.C.) to 2500 B.C., to learn about various foods in eastern North America and how to exploit them.

   This is simply not true. The Koster people knew their food resources intimately and did a superb job of feeding their communities. During the occupation of Horizon 11, Early Archaic people had developed a highly selective exploitation pattern of subsistence. They were not just taking foods randomly from the landscape. Rather, they calculated how to provide the community with the most nutritious foods possible while expending the least effort. In addition to deer and smaller mammals, they ate large quantities of fish, freshwater mussels, and nuts. Fish and nuts—in addition to being available each year, and easy to take in large quantities—are highly complementary components of a nutritious diet. Nuts contain fat for high energy, which many freshwater fish lack. The kind of input–output analysis which was taking place was worthy of the most sophisticated culture.

   Here's a sample note card for a *quotation* of an important portion of that passage:

Quotation Note Card

(D)

(C) St7

Sophisticated Food Gathering by 6400 B.C.

(A) "During the occupation of Horizon 11, Early Archaic people had developed a highly selective exploitation pattern of subsistence. They were not just taking foods randomly from the landscape."

(p.244) (B)

What to include on a quotation note card:

A. Put *quotation marks* around quoted material.

B. Put the page number (here, p. 244) in parentheses. If you are using a book that is part of a multivolume set but that doesn't have a separate title, include the volume number like this: (3:172).

C. The *code number* shows that this is the seventh card made from the Struever and Holton book. Using the bibliography code (St) from the bibliography card makes it unnecessary to put complete bibliographic information on each note card, and the number added (to make St7) provides a code that distinguishes this note card from others from the same book. In Chapter 20 we'll show you another way to use the code number. For now, keep all note cards from the same work together.

D. *Optional.* Use key word headings that might help you later to arrange the facts and ideas and to make sure you have enough support.

If you had *summarized* the entire passage, condensing the original material into a shorter version in your own words, the card would look like this:

Summary Note Card

St.7

Sophisticated Food Gathering by 6400 B.C.

Ⓐ — Contrary to the belief that prehistoric Indians needed some 6,000 to 9,000 years to adapt to using foods native to North America, the Koster discoveries indicate that by 6400 B.C.

Ⓑ — (4,000 years earlier than commonly accepted), the early Indians were choosing the high-quality foods that would support the entire population and that could be gathered easily.   (p.244)

What's different about a summary note card?

A. *No quotation marks.* Of course, even though you don't borrow the exact words, you do borrow the idea, and you must give credit for it (see Chapter 20).

B.   Your own words but the author's ideas. More important than reducing the length of the original, with a summary you mentally
"process" the material, capturing the idea or facts and making yourself more knowledgeable about your topic. Notice that the comment in parentheses within the summary above is an *interpretation*
of the evidence in the original, demonstrating that the writer of the
note card has processed the passage.

A *paraphrase,* too, is a retelling of the original in your own words.
But a paraphrase is different from a summary: The paraphrase tends to
follow the sentence-by-sentence pattern of the original more closely and
also is about the same length as the original. Use paraphrase note cards
sparingly. If you're going to take notes that closely follow the original,
why not quote instead? Then you'll have the exact words in case you decide to quote all or part of the passage in your paper. Still, a paraphrase is
useful when the original is technical or complex or when it isn't worded
well—then the paraphrase can help simplify or "interpret" the original. If
we paraphrase the two sentences quoted in the sample quotation note
card on p. 154, the paraphrase would look like this:

Paraphrase Note Card

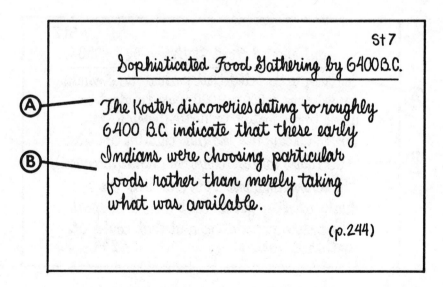

What's special about the paraphrase note card?

A.   We restated the quotation in our own words, so there are no
quotation marks.

B. The paraphrase interprets the technical wording from the original: "highly selective exploitation pattern of subsistence" in the original has been simplified to "choosing particular foods."

HOW TO GO WRONG

Most of the problems with taking notes come with paraphrases and summaries. If you're putting the original into your own words and you want to retain wording from the original, you must use quotation marks. What if you had written something like this?

For many years archaeologists have assumed that the prehistoric Indians needed several thousand years to discover how to exploit the various foods in eastern North America, but the Koster Indians had learned to be highly selective in their food choices rather than just taking foods randomly from the landscape.

This looks like a paraphrase or summary, right? Right. It *looks* like one, but it's an unacknowledged, loose quotation. It should have looked like this:

For many years "archaeologists have assumed" that the prehistoric Indians needed "several thousand years" to discover "how to exploit" the "various foods in eastern North America," but the Koster Indians had learned to be "highly selective" in their food choices rather than "just taking foods randomly from the landscape."

Of course, that looks peculiar. No thought has been given here to choosing effective portions of the original for a quotation—rather, the use of key words from the original appears to be accidental.

You *can* mix quotation with summary or paraphrase, but be selective in the quotation part. And keep this rule in mind: Whenever you use another author's words, put them in quotation marks. Failure to do so is dishonest.

HOW MANY NOTE CARDS?

So far so good, but how many note cards do you need to make? There is no easy answer; some subjects demand more support than others. A reliable way of telling when you have enough support is to compare your notes with a working outline of your paper. The next chapter will say more about your paper's outline. For now just remember this: You don't have to wait until you've finished with note-taking to begin organizing a working outline. You can revise and expand the outline as you find new material. At the same time, though, the working outline can direct your research by helping you see gaps in your support material. When you've filled all the gaps, you can be comfortable that you have taken enough notes.

SOME FINE POINTS

Be careful to quote accurately. Do not correct mistakes you find an author has made. If he is wrong about a date—for example, if he says that Pearl Harbor was attacked the wrong year—you show that you know better like this: "When the Imperial Air Forces of Japan attacked Pearl Harbor on 7 December 1940 [*sic*], they demonstrated how vulnerable ships were to surprise air attack." The [*sic*] in brackets, not parentheses, is a Latin word meaning *thus.* In formal writing we use it to mean "I have written it that way intentionally to show that the author used those precise words."

If you want to omit some words from a quotation, show the omission with three dots (space between each one). But be careful not to leave out words like *not* or *never* which would significantly change the meaning. If the words you omit come at the end of a sentence, use the three-dot ellipsis and then punctuate normally:

... in fourteen cases....

... but when...?

Keep all the note cards from the same source together at this stage of the research and writing process. If you left a page number or a quotation mark off a note card, it will be much easier to find if all your cards are together.

EXERCISES

A.   In 1821 Thomas Jefferson began his *Autobiography.* The paragraph below comes from page 54 of an edition published in 1909 by the New York firm of Henry and Sons. In the library it has call number E 332.9 A8.

The first establishment in Virginia which became permanent, was made in 1607. I have found no mention of negroes in the colony until about 1650. The first brought here as slaves were by a Dutch ship; after which the English commenced the trade, and continued it until the revolutionary war. That suspended, *ipso facto,* their further importation for the present, and the business of the war pressing constantly on the legistlature, this subject was not acted on finally until the year '78, when I brought in a bill to prevent their further importation. This passed without opposition, and stopped the increase of the evil by importation, leaving to future efforts its final eradication.

1. Make a bibliography card for Jefferson's *Autobiography.*

2. Select at least three lines of the paragraph and prepare a note card quoting directly from the paragraph.

3. Prepare a summary of the entire passage; use no more than three lines of your own words to do it.

4. Now paraphrase the lines you quoted in exercise A2.

5. A final check:
    Did you put a code number on the bibliography card?
    Did you use that code on the note cards?
    Is the library call number on the bibliography card?
    Did you put quotation marks where needed?

B. In the government-publication section of the library you find a book called *The Navajo Nation: An American Colony* which the United States Commission on Civil Rights published in Washington, D.C., in 1975. Its library call number is CR 1.2: N22/2. As you write a paper on the Navajo school systems which the whites operate, you find this paragraph (pp. 126–27):

> Navajos, in fact, have been excluded from the decisionmaking process in these school systems. The result has been a variety of educational policies unrelated to the Navajo community. The Navajo language and culture have been largely ignored in the curriculum offered to Navajo students. Although an occasional course in the Navajo language is offered, there is little push to develop bilingual education and some schools still reprimand students and teachers for speaking Navajo. Nor has bicultural education had much support from non-Indian educational planners on the reservation. Insensitivity to Navajo culture is revealed dramatically in the preservation by many schools of a dress code requiring male students to keep their hair short, effectively preventing them from wearing the traditional "Navajo knot."

1. Make a bibliography card for this book.

2. Prepare a note card quoting directly from the paragraph.

3. Prepare a summary of the entire passage; use no more than three lines of your own words to do it.

4. Now paraphrase the lines you quoted in Exercise B2.

5. A final check:
    Did you put a code number on your bibliography card?
    Did you use that code on the note cards?
    Is the library call number on the bibliography card?
    Did you put quotation marks where needed?

CHAPTER 20

Using Borrowed Material in Your Paper

AN OUTLINE

As we mentioned in the last chapter, you don't need to wait until you've finished taking all your notes to begin organizing that new knowledge. Develop an outline early and revise and expand it as you learn more. The working outline helps you discover gaps in your support, thereby suggesting areas for continued research. And the research suggests ways to modify the organization. In other words, you need to work back and forth between note-taking and outlining—each influences the other.

How do you begin organizing the support? By thinking. List all the *key* ideas you've discovered about your topic; just jot down the key words. Now, does a pattern of organization suggest itself? Would chronological order work? How about cause and effect or some of the other patterns you studied in Part IV? Once you've settled on the basic arrangement, fill in this outline, using as few words as you can without sacrificing clarity. Of course, you may not need exactly three major topics with three support ideas for each one. This is just a basic model.

    I.   Introduction (as a minimum, write the thesis of the paper):

   II.   First major topic:

       A. Support idea:

       B. Support idea:

       C. Support idea:

  III.   Second major topic:

       A. Support idea:

   B. Support idea:

   C. Support idea:

IV. Third major topic:

   A. Support idea:

   B. Support idea:

   C. Support idea:

 V. Conclusion:

The outline should look familiar, for it's the same basic pattern you've seen before. The major difference is that the outline here represents a greater amount of material, but the organizing process is the same.

What you have just done is to prepare a working outline, one that shows the way your paper looks so far. Your outline simply reduces a large quantity of information to its bare skeleton—just the main ideas and key support. This outline is merely a tool to show logically and clearly the relationships among the main ideas in the paper. It will help you discover gaps in support, indicating where you need to work more in research. And as you write a draft of your paper, it will help you remember the key ideas while you are filling in the details.

A TIMESAVER

Once you've prepared an outline, you're ready to assemble your detailed support. Arrange your note cards to follow your outline. Use the floor, your desk top, your roommate's bed, whatever you need to spread the cards out so you can see how they fill out the skeleton. Don't let your outline keep you from moving cards around. That outline is not engraved in bronze; you can alter it as you need to. But laying out your cards will help you see where the outline may be incomplete or where you need more information. You probably will have more note cards than you can use. Don't throw any away; you may find a place for them later.

When you are satisfied with the outline and its support, start writing. You may begin at the beginning with an introduction, then on to the first major topic, then the second, and so on. Many writers do it this way, and it may work for you. Or you may decide to start with the first major topic, go on to the next topics, and finish writing with the conclusion—

and then the introduction. Many other writers do it this way. The reason is simple: frequently you're not sure what you're going to say until you've said it. You actually discover what you think as you write because the ideas take over and lead you to new discoveries. If you have already written the introduction, you may find it has little relationship to what you finally say.

Regardless of where you start writing, you'll have to use some of your note cards. If you're using a quotation, here's a trick that can save you some work: In writing your draft, when you come to a place for a quotation note card, don't copy it again. Just paper-clip the quotation note card in place or leave room in your draft and write in the code number for the note card (remember the code number St7 we used on p. 155?). Doing it this way will save you writing and will help keep the quotations accurate, no matter how many drafts you go through. A caution: this trick isn't intended for use with summaries and paraphrases; those notes already are in your own words, and you should be weaving the ideas and facts into the fabric of your writing in the paper's draft.

USING BORROWED MATERIAL SKILLFULLY

Skilled use of borrowed material is one mark of an accomplished writer. You can't expect just to sprinkle it on the paper in the hope it will magically create an argument for you. Good arguments with borrowed material supporting them don't just happen; they come from careful work. To make sure your borrowed material helps your argument, you must consider two key questions: whether to quote or not, and what to quote from. Answers to these questions are closely related and depend on the paper you're writing.

USING PRIMARY SOURCES

If you are writing about Lincoln's assassination, you should go to some of the primary sources—eyewitness accounts, newspaper articles of the time, official investigations—and quote directly from them. For example, you might quote from this paragraph in the *Diary of Gideon Welles*, Lincoln's Secretary of the Navy, to show the confusion surrounding the assassination:

> I had retired to bed about half past-ten on the evening of the 14th of April, and was just getting asleep when Mrs. Welles, my wife, said some one was at our door. Sitting up in bed, I heard a voice

twice call to John, my son, whose sleeping-room was on the second floor directly over the front entrance. I arose at once and raised a window, when my messenger, James Smith, called to me that Mr. Lincoln, the President, had been shot, and said Secretary Seward and his son, Assistant Secretary Frederick Seward, were assassinated. James was much alarmed and excited. I told him his story was very incoherent and improbable, that he was associating men who were not together, and liable to attack at the same time. "Where," I inquired, "was the President when shot?" James said he was at Ford's Theatre on 10th Street. "Well," said I, "Secretary Seward is an invalid in bed in his house yonder on 15th Street." James said he had been there, stopped in at the house to make inquiry before alarming me.[1]

This is a *primary* source, one that directly resulted from the events you're writing about. Other primary sources include novels or poems for papers on literary topics, census or economic reports for history or business papers, and official documents or reports for history and many other kinds of papers.

USING SECONDARY SOURCES

A *secondary* source is different; although it talks about events, its material comes not from the event itself but from primary sources or other secondary sources. John Cottrell's *Anatomy of an Assassination,* from which we quote on p. 165, is a secondary source about Lincoln's death. Other examples of secondary sources are criticism of a novel, a history of the United States, or an article about a historical figure.

Look at these two lists to see the difference:

Primary source	Secondary source
The Panama Canal Treaty printed in the *Congressional Record*	An article about the Panama Canal Treaty in *Time*
Shakespeare's Sonnet 73	A book about Shakespeare's sonnets
An 1865 newspaper article about Lincoln's assassins	A 1966 book about Lincoln's assassination

As a general guide, quote directly from primary sources to give examples, a flavor of the time, or some specific well-chosen words. Paraphrase

[1] Gideon Welles, *Diary of Gideon Welles* (Boston: Houghton Mifflin, 1911), II, 283–84.

or summarize secondary sources to cite a respected authority, to sum up trends, or to give your paper a starting point. But whether you use primary or secondary sources, whether you quote or paraphrase or summarize, you must follow three steps to use borrowed material effectively: *introduce* the borrowed material, *present* it, and *credit* the source.

INTRODUCING BORROWED MATERIAL

Perhaps the most neglected step in using borrowed material is the first one—introducing it. In this step you mention the author or title of the work before beginning the quotation, to signal to your reader that you are quoting. Here are some sample introductions:

As Emerson says in his Journals, "...."

According to the press secretary, the President decided that "...."

Senator Phogbreath was right when he said, "...."

In her book *Shakespeare of London,* Marchette Chute reveals, "...."

The variety of introductions is almost endless, but all of them let your reader see whether the source you're citing is reputable. Without an introduction, the quotation seems just spliced in; look for such an example in the following paragraph:

President Lincoln's second inauguration was cause for great celebration among his supporters. On the eve of the inauguration, many friends attended riotous public and private parties. Even the new Vice-President, Andrew Johnson, at one time a poor tailor's boy from Tennessee, was drunk the next morning at his swearing in. "Flushed and fortified with three large whiskies, he shuffled into the Senate Chamber...."[2] As a result of Johnson's drunkenness, President Lincoln refused to see him again until Good Friday, 1865, the day Lincoln was assassinated.

Every reader will wonder who described Johnson or where the quotation came from. It seems to be just dropped into the paragraph. Annoying, isn't it? Don't annoy your readers by sending them to your notes to find out who said what you've quoted; don't even leave them slightly frustrated from wondering about it. Introduce the material:

[2]John Cottrell, *Anatomy of an Assassination* (London: Muller, 1966), p. 45.

... his swearing in. In his *Anatomy of an Assassination*, English historian John Cottrell describes Johnson this way: "Flushed and fortified with three large whiskies, he shuffled into the Senate Chamber...."[3]

This way, your reader knows who said what you've quoted and where you found it; the footnote gives the complete data to find the book if your reader should want to.

The introduction is even more important for a summary or paraphrase than it is for a direct quotation. We can all tell where a quotation begins by the quotation marks. But where does the paraphrase begin here?

Despite the bitterness of the campaign, Lincoln's friends and supporters had many public and private celebrations to mark his second inauguration. Just before noon of inauguration day, the results of the celebration were scandalously made public to the embarrassed congress. Stumbling and shuffling, the new Vice-President, Andrew Johnson, "a one-time illiterate" tailor's helper from Tennessee, staggered into the Senate Chamber. He was drunk from the after-effects of a party given by the Senate clerk.[4]

How many of the ideas came from Cottrell's book? Where does the paraphrase begin? At the first word of the paragraph? At the quotation? Is the entire paragraph a paraphrase? Who knows? But when you introduce the paraphrase, everyone will know:

... Just before noon of inauguration day, *according to historian John Cottrell*, the results of the celebration were scandalously ... the Senate clerk.[4]

With just that simple introduction, you've let your reader know where your paraphrasing begins. (Be sure to introduce your summaries as well.)

PRESENTING BORROWED MATERIAL

You've already seen many examples of how to present the material you borrow. Here are some tips:
• After you introduce borrowed material, use quotation marks if it is a direct quotation.

[3]Cottrell, p. 45.
[4]Cottrell, p. 45.

• Don't quote more than you need to make your point; don't quote two sentences if one says what you need.

• Don't quote a full sentence if part of one will do.

The quotations we've seen so far have all been fairly short, four lines or less. Sometimes you'll need longer quotations (more than four typed lines in your paper). For example, if you're trying to demonstrate that a novelist's style interferes with his story, you might want to quote a whole paragraph or two. Here's how to do it:

> In *Deerslayer*, James Fenimore Cooper always intrudes into the story with wordy authorial comment:
>
>> Deerslayer made no answer; but he stood leaning on his rifle, gazing at the view which so much delighted him. The reader is not to suppose, however, that it was the pic-turesque alone which so strongly attracted his attention. The spot was lovely, of a truth, and it was then seen in one of its favorable moments, the surface of the lake being as smooth as glass, and as limpid as pure air, throwing back the mountains, clothed in dark pines along the whole of its eastern boundary, the points throwing forward their trees even to nearly horizontal lines, while the bays were seen glittering through an occasional arch beneath, left by a vault fretted with branches and leaves.[5]

Here are the details on how to quote if the borrowed material is more than four typed lines in your paper:

Triple-space from the last line of your text.

Indent ten spaces from the left margin.

Type single-spaced.

Do not use quotation marks (unless you are quoting dialogue which has quotation marks).

Do not indent the first line of the quotation unless it begins a para-graph; then indent three additional spaces (a total of thirteen spaces from left margin).

Triple-space to the next part of your text.

One way to think about using a long quotation is to imagine that you simply clip it out of the original and retype it the way it is. You add no

---

[5] James Fenimore Cooper, *The Deerslayer* (n.p.: T. Nelson, n.d.), p. 31.

quotation marks (though you may use ellipsis or *sic* if needed) or any other changes except to block-indent it. The indention indicates that you are quoting.

But remember, like a short quotation, the long one needs an introduction, too. In fact, the introduction to a long quotation often tells the reader what you expect him to notice about it, thus giving him the right perspective. In our last example, we told you to watch for Cooper's wordy authorial comment.

CREDITING YOUR SOURCE

Whenever you use borrowed material, the third step is also essential: *crediting your source*. You must identify the printed or spoken source of your information. Not to do so is dishonest, a form of cheating.

You can give credit to your sources in two simple ways—with notes or with parenthetical information. Usually parenthetical notations, which are included *in* the text of the paper, aren't used to provide as much information as would be included in a note at the foot of the page or at the end of the paper. A parenthetical source note might look like this (*Time*, 3 Sep. 1977, p. 47) or (*The History of the Middle Earth*, Holt, 1973, p. 432). Because they're inserted into the body of the paper, parenthetical references clutter up the writing and interfere with the smooth flow of ideas. To prevent that interference, use notes.

A note simply puts all the necessary publication information—the credit to your source—in a note at the foot of the page or at the end of your paper. You signal your reader that the note is there by putting a number raised *a half line* after the last quoted or borrowed matter, like this:[1].

The next chapter will show you in detail the kinds of notes you will need most often.

EXERCISES

A. Questions.

   1. Explain the difference between primary source and secondary source. Give an example of each.

   _____

   _____

   _____

_____

_____

2. What are the three key steps for using borrowed material skill-fully?

_____

_____

_____

B. In 1878 Jakob Burckhardt published his famous work *The Civiliza-tion of the Renaissance in Italy.* In the chapter titled "Equality of Men and Women" Burckhardt has this paragraph:

> The education given to women in the upper classes was essen-tially the same as that given to men. The Italian, at the time of the Renaissance, felt no scruple in putting sons and daughters alike under the same course of literary and even philological instruction. Indeed, looking at this ancient culture as the chief treasure of life, he was glad that girls should have a share in it. We have seen what perfection was attained by the daughters of princely houses in writing and speaking Latin. Many others must at least have been able to read it, in order to follow the conversation of the day, which turned largely on classical subjects.

Now, quote two sentences from Burckhardt. Remember to intro-duce the quotation and to quote accurately. For this exercise, don't worry about crediting your source.

_____

_____

_____

_____

_____

_____

C. In the *Federalist,* No. 47, published in the *New York Packet,* 1 Febru-ary 1788, James Madison, later President of the United States, wrote, "The accumulation of all powers, legislative, executive, and judiciary, in the same hands, whether of one, a few, or many, and whether heredi-tary, self-appointed or elective may justly be pronounced the very defini-tion of tyranny."

1. Prepare a direct quotation in which you omit a phrase or two. Show omission with an ellipsis. Be sure to introduce the quotation.

_____

_____

_____

_____

_____

_____

_____

2. Prepare a paraphrase and introduce it.

_____

_____

_____

_____

_____

_____

_____

CHAPTER 21

Notes

Whether you use quotations, paraphrases, or summaries, you must give the sources of your information in notes. In Part III you learned a make-shift system that let the reader know whenever you were using outside sources for support. This chapter presents a better system, one that not only tells your reader that you are using borrowed material but also gives him enough information to find the source.

The formats for notes in this chapter and for bibliography in the next one (Chapter 22) generally follow the *MLA Handbook*, published by the Modern Language Association. This handbook is an accepted standard for documentation in many academic fields. Other widely used style guides include Kate Turabian's *A Manual for Writers* and the University of Chicago Press' *A Manual of Style*. You should keep in mind that there are minor differences in style among the various manuals and use caution when you switch from one style guide to another.

PLACING YOUR NOTES

You may put *footnotes* at the bottom of the page to which they refer. When you type a paper with footnotes at the bottom of the page, do it like this:

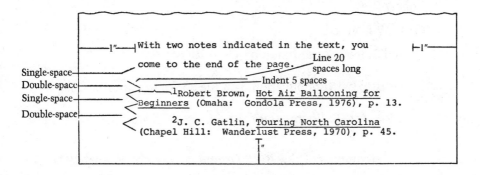

A far simpler way, and the one we recommend, is to put all your notes together on one or two pages at the end of your paper, like this:

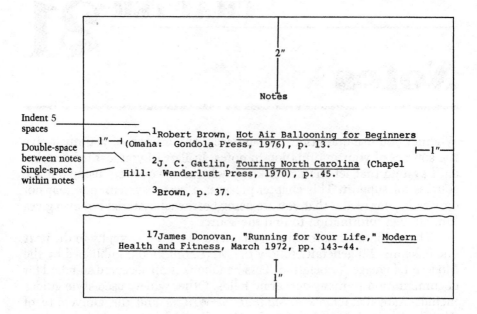

WHAT NOTES ARE

Every footnote (at the bottom of the page) or endnote (at the end of the paper) should lead a reader to a specific page from which you have borrowed. To do that, each note has three basic parts, each joined by a comma:

1. The name of the person or group responsible (author, speaker, or editor) with the name in the normal order:

Robert Brown,

G. T. Wilson, ed.,

United States Commission on Civil Rights,

2. The title (with publication data for books in parentheses):

Hot Air Ballooning for Beginners (Omaha: Gondola Press, 1976),

"Melodramas of the 70s," *Drama in Review*, 8 Aug. 1977,

The Navajo Nation: An American Colony (Washington, D.C.: GPO, 1975),

3. The *specific* page or pages in the book or article from which you have borrowed:

p. 13.

pp. 123–34.

pp. 321, 358, 402.

If we put the three parts together, we get this form:

```
            1
 ┌──────────────┐┌────────────────────────────────────────
 ¹Robert Brown, Hot Air Ballooning for Beginners (Omaha:
 ┌──────────────────┐┌────────────┐
       2                    3
 Gondola Press, 1976), p. 13.
```

All footnotes or endnotes follow this three-part pattern, though the details vary depending upon the book or article. If you remember that a comma connects each of the three parts, and what each of the parts contains, you should have no trouble handling variations from the basic form. To help you, we have examples of the most common kinds of notes you'll use. Bibliography entries to match them appear in the next chapter.

MODEL NOTES: BOOKS

A. To a book with one author:

¹Robert Brown, *Hot Air Ballooning for Beginners* (Omaha: Gondola Press, 1976), p. 13.

B. To a book with two authors or more:

²R. J. Eden, P. V. Landshoff, D. I. Olive, and J. C. Polkinghorne, *The Analytic S-Matrix* (Cambridge: Cambridge Univ. Press, 1966), p. 79.

Cite all authors' names as they appear on the title page.

C. To a modern reprint of an earlier edition:

³Dunn Bradlane, *How to Choose Stocks* (1929; rpt. Foxglove: Northern Wyoming State College, 1974), pp. 104–09.

D. To a book edited by someone other than the author:

⁴Captain John Smith, *Travels and Works of Captain John Smith, President of Virginia, and Admiral of New England, 1580– 1631,* ed. Edward Arber and A. G. Bradley (Edinburgh: n.p., 1910), p. 124.

E. To a book that is part of a multivolume work:

⁵Allan Nevins, *The Organized War to Victory,* Vol. IV of *The War for the Union* (New York: Charles Scribner's Sons, 1971), pp. 127–28.

F. To an edition other than the first:

⁶James Bolen, *In Search of Our Ancestors,* 3rd ed. (Arlington, Va.: Burning Tree Press, 1981), pp. 231–32.

G. To a story or essay in a collection:

⁷Ernest Hemingway, "A Clean, Well-Lighted Place," in *Studies in the Short Story,* ed. Virgil Scott, alt. ed. (New York: Holt, Rinehart and Winston, 1971), p. 336.

Alt. ed. abbreviates alternate edition.

H. To an anonymous book:

⁸*Confessions of a Pusher* (Chicago: Needle Press, 1963), pp. 122 –31.
⁹*Who's Who in the West, 1977–78,* 16th ed. (Chicago: Marquis, 1977), II, 433.

Cite such books in notes and bibliography by title, not by "Anon." or "Anonymous."

I. To a translation:

¹⁰Dante Alighieri, *The Inferno,* trans. John Ciardi (New York: Signet, 1954), p. 59.

J. To an introduction:

¹¹Kenneth Myrick, Introd., *Merchant of Venice,* by William Shakespeare, in *The Complete Signet Classic Shakespeare,* ed. Sylvan Barnet (New York: Harcourt Brace Jovanovich, 1972), p. 599.
¹²James A. Work, Introd., *Tristram Shandy,* by Laurence Sterne (New York: Odyssey Press, 1940), p. xxi.

Substitute Preface, Foreword, Afterword as appropriate.

K. To an article in a reference book:

[13]Richard N. Current, "Lincoln, Abraham," *Encyclopaedia Britannica*, 1969 ed., p. 52.

Cite page number if you are citing only one page from a multipage article. Otherwise omit it.

L. To a book with a corporate author:

[14]United States Commission on Civil Rights, *A Guide to Federal Laws Prohibiting Sex Discrimination* (Washington, D.C.: GPO, 1976), p. 7.

M. A book that doesn't show place or date of publication, publisher, or page number:

Indicate missing data with these abbreviations:

no place of publication given: n.p.
(n.p.: Golden Grenich Press, 1978), p. 18.

no publisher given: n.p.
(Boston: n.p., 1969), p. 31.

no date given: n.d.
(New Haven: Yale U.P., n.d.), pp. 111–21.

no page numbers: n.pag.
(Oxford: Blackwell, 1912), n.pag.

If you learn unlisted data from another source, such as the card catalog, include it in brackets:
(Boston: [Blue Book Press], 1969), p. 31.

Use as many abbreviations as needed to indicate incomplete data:
(n.p.: n.p., 1918), n.pag.

N. Second and later references to a book already cited:

Use author's last name and page number:

[15]Brown, p. 24.

If the same author wrote two or more works you are using, give his last name, a short title, and page number.

[16]Brown, *Hot Air Ballooning*, p. 27.

[17]Brown, *Surviving a Crash Landing*, p. 4.

If the book has no author listed, use a short title instead:

[18]*Confessions,* p. 138.

MODEL NOTES:
ARTICLES IN PERIODICALS

First, some special rules for periodical articles:
- put article titles in quotation marks
- put periodical title in italics by underscoring on the typewriter or under-
lining in pen
- for journals, use arabic numerals for volume numbers:
—if pagination is continued throughout the year, use the volume number (year), page number:

Southern Quarterly, 14 (1977), 380.

—if each issue of the journal is paged independently, use the volume
number (month or season, year), page number:

Physical Therapy Journal, 31 (Jan. 1973), 56.

- for newspapers and weekly or monthly magazines, do not use the volume
number: give the complete date (month may be abbreviated), page
number:

New York Times, 24 Feb. 1979, p. 4.

- use p. or pp. for page numbers only if no volume number appears.

A. To a daily newspaper article:

[19]Phil McCombs, "RVs and Bikes—Lifestyles in Motion,"
Washington Star, 4 Sep. 1977, Sec. A, p. 1.

If the author isn't listed, begin the footnote with the article title.

B. To a weekly newspaper or magazine article:

[20]Horace Sutton, "What Makes Britain Great No Matter What,"
Saturday Review, 11 June 1977, p. 7.
[21]"EEC Members Not in the Mood for Compromise," *The German Tribune,* 10 July 1977, p. 1.

C. To an article in a monthly magazine:

[22]Eleanor Holmes Norton, "The Woman Who Changed the South," *Ms.*, July 1977, p. 51.

D. To an article in a journal with continuous pagination:

[23]Robert Bledsoe, "Kubrick's 'Vanity Fair,'" *Rocky Mountain Review*, 31 (1977), 96.

E. To an article in a journal that is paged separately each issue:

[24]Marion Montgomery, "The Pursuit of the Worthy: Thomas Hardy's Greekness in *Jude the Obscure*," *The Denver Quarterly*, 1, No. 4 (1967), 31.

F. To an article in a journal with more than one series:

[25]Barbara A. Wise, "Married Half a Life," *Ohio Historical Papers*, NS 4 (1979), 104.

Use NS for new series and OS for old series.

G. To an anonymous article:

[26]"Report Finds US Academic Research Base is Endangered," *Physics Today*, Aug. 1977, p. 61.

H. To a letter to an editor:

[27]J. D. McFarland, Letter, *Western Law Review*, 63 (1978), 32–33.

I. To a review:

[28]Michael Irvin, "This Island Now," rev. of *The Ice Age*, by Margaret Drabble, *Times Literary Supplement*, 2 Sep. 1977, p. 1045.
[29]Erika Lindemann, rev. of *English Schools in the Middle Ages*, by Nicholas Orme, *Shakespeare Studies*, 9 (1976), 357.

J. To an article with a quotation in the title:

[30]Frederick Buell, " 'To be quiet in the hands of the marvelous': The Poetry of A. R. Ammons," *Iowa Review*, 8 (1977), 68.

Subsequent references to an article follow the format shown for books, sample note numbers 15, 16, 17, or 18.

MODEL NOTES: OTHER SOURCES

A. To a lecture:

   [31]Giles E. Dawson, "Elizabethan Marriage in Fiction and Fact," Folger Lecture Series, Washington, D.C., 12 Dec. 1977.

   Give the name, "title (if you know it)," organization, location, and date.

B. To a film:

   [32]Roy Fettucini, dir., *Gidget Goes to Forest Lawn,* with Dixie Lee and Stanley Dennis, United Artists, 1979.

C. To a television or radio program:

   [33]*The Streets of Laredo,* dir. William Cody, CBS Adventure Theater, 4 July 1978.

D. Recordings:

   [34]Randall Jarrell, "The Ball-Turret Gunner," *Poems against War,* Caedmon, TC 1363, 1971.

E. Personal interview:

   [35]Personal interview with Janet Hiller, 5 Jan. 1981.
   [36]Telephone interview with Henry Kissinger, 18 Feb. 1982.

F. Class handout or lecture notes:

   [37]"Organizing Principles," English 350 handout, Southern Arizona State College, 4 May 1978.

EXERCISE

Prepare a notes page with the following entries:
1. A note to p. 131 of the book by Maynard Mack on p. 142.
2. A note for the quotation from Thomas Jefferson in Exercise A of Chapter 19, p. 158.
3. A note for the quotation for *The Navajo Nation* in Exercise B of Chapter 19, p. 159.
4. A second note to the Mack book, this time to p. 146.

5.   A note for an article appearing in the *El Paso Gazette* on 28 February 1979, called "Gas Crisis Looming—Again"; the story was written by R. P. McMurphy and appeared on p. 24.

6.   A note to p. 172 of Justin G. Schiller's article called "Annual Report of Librarian of Congress"; the article appeared on pp. 163–73 of a periodical called *AB Bookman's Weekly* on 12 January 1976.

CHAPTER 22

Bibliography

A bibliography is the final and easiest step in preparing a research paper. Unlike the notes page, the bibliography is in alphabetical order so the reader can have a convenient list of all the works you used in your paper.

WHAT TO DO

Take all the working bibliography cards for sources you actually have used for your research (but not for sources you glanced at and tossed aside) and put them in alphabetical order by author's last name—or by title if the author is not listed. If you prepared your working bibliography cards with the correct formats for bibliographic entries, all that's left is to write the bibliography carefully and type it. If your working bibliography cards aren't in the correct formats, then put the information in proper order as you write the bibliography page. In either case, the typed page should look like this:

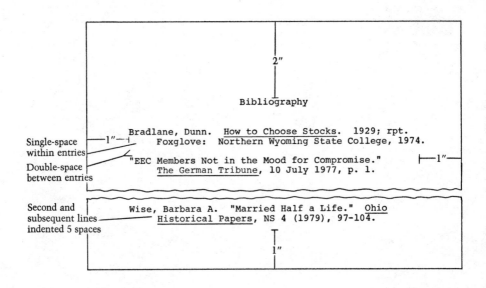

WHAT A BIBLIOGRAPHY ENTRY IS

An entry in your bibliography is another part of the way you credit your source; with a note, it completes the third step in using borrowed material. Like the note, each entry consists of three major parts, this time separated by periods:

1. The *name* of the person responsible (author, speaker, or editor), in reverse order for alphabetizing:

Brown, Robert.

Wilson, G. T., ed.

U.S. Commission on Civil Rights.

2. The *title* of the article or book:

Hot Air Ballooning for Beginners.

"Melodramas of the 70s."

The Navajo Nation: An American Colony.

3. The *publication* data. For articles, this part of the entry includes the name of the magazine or journal, volume, date, and page numbers. For books, this part includes place, publisher, and date, none of which appears in parenthesis:

Omaha: Gondola Press, 1976.

Drama in Review, 8 Aug. 1977, pp. 122–47.

Washington, D.C.: GPO, 1975.

When we put the parts together we get this form:

Brown, Robert. *Hot Air Ballooning for Beginners.* Omaha: Gondola Press, 1976.

Wilson, G. T., ed. "Melodramas of the 70s." *Drama in Review,* 8 Aug. 1977, pp. 122–47.

U.S. Commission on Civil Rights. *The Navajo Nation: An American Colony.* Washington, D.C.: GPO, 1975.

Although the bibliography entry consists of three basic parts (like the note), several differences mark the bibliography entry:

1. The author's name is *reversed,* last name first, for alphabetizing.

2. Each part of the entry is separated by a *period.*
3. The first line of the entry is *extended to the left five spaces.*
To help you see the differences, we have listed model bibliography entries below; they correspond to the notes in Chapter 21.

MODEL BIBLIOGRAPHY ENTRIES: BOOKS

A. For a book with one author (see note 1*):

Brown, Robert. *Hot Air Ballooning for Beginners.* Omaha: Gondola Press, 1976.

B. For a book with two or more authors (see note 2):

Eden, R. J., P. V. Landshoff, D. I. Olive, and J. C. Polkinghorne. *The Analytic S-Matrix.* Cambridge: Cambridge Univ. Press, 1966.

C. For a modern reprint of an earlier edition (see note 3):

Bradlane, Dunn. *How to Choose Stocks.* 1929; rpt. Foxglove: Northern Wyoming State College, 1974.

D. For a book edited by someone other than the author (see note 4):

Smith, Captain John. *Travels and Works of Captain John Smith, President of Virginia, and Admiral of New England, 1580–1631.* Ed. Edward Arber and A. G. Bradley. Edinburgh: n.p., 1910.

E. For a book that is part of a multivolume work (see note 5):

Nevins, Allan. *The Organized War to Victory.* Vol. IV of *The War for the Union.* New York: Charles Scribner's Sons, 1971.

Note that this entry has *four* parts separated by periods.
F. For an edition other than the first (see note 6):

Bolen, James. *In Search of Our Ancestors.* 3rd ed. Arlington, Va.: Burning Tree Press, 1981.

---

* Note numbers refer to the notes on pp. 173–178 in the previous chapter.

G. For a short story or essay contained in a collection (see note 7):

> Hemingway, Ernest. "A Clean, Well-Lighted Place." In *Studies in the Short Story.* Ed. Virgil Scott. Alt. ed. New York: Holt, Rinehart and Winston, 1971, pp. 335–38.

H. For an anonymous book (see notes 8 and 9):

> *Confessions of a Pusher.* Chicago: Needle Press, 1963.

> *Who's Who in the West, 1977–78.* 16th ed. 2 vols. Chicago: Marquis, 1977.

I. For a translation (see note 10):

> Alighieri, Dante. *The Inferno.* Trans. John Ciardi. New York: Signet, 1954.

J. For an introduction to a book (see notes 11 and 12):

> Myrick, Kenneth, introd. *Merchant of Venice.* By William Shakespeare. In *The Complete Signet Classic Shakespeare.* Ed. Sylvan Barnet. New York: Harcourt Brace Jovanovich, 1972, pp. 599–603.

Page numbers refer to the pages occupied by the Introduction.

> Work, James A., introd. *Tristram Shandy.* By Laurence Sterne. New York: Odyssey Press, pp. i–lxxv.

K. For an entry in a reference book (see note 13):

> Current, Richard N. "Lincoln, Abraham." *Encyclopaedia Britannica.* 1969 ed.

L. For a book with a corporate author (see note 14):

> U.S. Commission on Civil Rights. *A Guide to Federal Laws Prohibiting Sex Discrimination.* Washington, D.C.: GPO, 1976.

M. For a book without place or date of publication, publisher, or page numbers (see page 175):

> *The Eloquent Forty-four.* Boston: n.p., 1969.

MODEL BIBLIOGRAPHY ENTRIES: ARTICLES

A. For a daily newspaper article (see note 19):

> McCombs, Phil. "RVs and Bikes—Lifestyles in Motion." *Washington Star*, 4 Sep. 1977, Sec. A, p. 1.

B. For a weekly newspaper or magazine article (see notes 20 and 21):

> "EEC Members Not in the Mood for Compromise." *The German Tribune*, 10 July 1977, p. 1.

> Sutton, Horace. "What Makes Britain Great No Matter What." *Saturday Review*, 11 June 1977, 6–7.

C. For an article in a monthly magazine (see note 22):

> Norton, Eleanor Holmes. "The Woman Who Changed the South." *Ms.*, July 1977, pp. 51, 98.

> Note that this article appeared on two widely separated pages.

D. For an article in a journal with continuous pagination throughout an entire volume, regardless of the number of issues or parts (see note 23):

> Bledsoe, Robert. "Kubrick's 'Vanity Fair.'" *Rocky Mountain Review*, 31 (1977), 96–99.

> Do not use p. or pp. after a volume number or after the year in parenthesis.

E. For an article in a journal that is paged separately each issue (see note 24):

> Montgomery, Marion. "The Pursuit of the Worthy: Thomas Hardy's Greekness in *Jude the Obscure*." *The Denver Quarterly*, 1, No. 4. (1967), 29–43.

F. For an article in a journal with more than one series (see note 25):

> Wise, Barbara A. "Married Half a Life." *Ohio Historical Papers*, NS 4 (1979), 97–104.

G. For an anonymous article (see note 26):

> "Report Finds US Academic Research Base is Endangered." *Physics Today*, Aug. 1977, pp. 61–62.

H. For a letter to the editor (see note 27):

McFarland, J. D. Letter. *Western Law Review*, 63 (1978), 32–33.

I. For a review (see notes 28 and 29):

Irvin, Michael. "This Island Now." Rev. of *The Ice Age*, by Margaret Drabble. *Times Literary Supplement*, 2 Sep. 1977, p. 1045.

Lindemann, Erika. Rev. of *English Schools in the Middle Ages*, by Nicholas Orme. *Shakespeare Studies*, 9 (1976), 355–57.

If no author is given, begin with Rev. of. . . .

J. For an article with a quotation in the title (see note 30):

Buell, Frederick. " 'To be quiet in the hands of the marvelous': The Poetry of A. R. Ammons." *Iowa Review*, 8 (1977), 64–72.

MODEL BIBLIOGRAPHY ENTRIES: OTHER SOURCES

A. For a lecture (see note 31):

Dawson, Giles E. "Elizabethan Marriage in Fiction and Fact." Folger Lecture Series, Washington, D.C., 12 Dec. 1977.

B. For a film (see note 32):

Fettucini, Roy, dir. *Gidget Goes to Forest Lawn.* With Dixie Lee and Stanley Dennis. United Artists, 1979.

C. For a television or radio program (see note 33):

The Streets of Laredo. Dir. William Cody, CBS Adventure Theater, 4 July 1978.

D. For a recording (see note 34):

Jarrell, Randall. "The Ball-Turret Gunner." *Poems against War.* Caedmon, TC 1363, 1971.

E. For a personal or telephone interview (see notes 35 and 36):

Hiller, Janet. Personal interview. 5 Jan. 1981.

Kissinger, Henry. Telephone interview. 18 Feb. 1982.

F. For a class handout or lecture notes (see note 37):

"Organizing Principles." English 350 handout, Southern Arizona
State College, 4 May 1978.

EXERCISE

Prepare a bibliography consisting of these books and articles:
1. The book by Maynard Mack cited on p. 142.
2. The book by Thomas Jefferson cited in Exercise A of Chapter 19, p. 158.
3. *The Navajo Nation*, cited in Exercise B of Chapter 19, p. 159.
4. An article appearing in the *El Paso Gazette* on February 28, 1979, called "Gas Crisis Looming—Again." This story was written by R. P. McMurphy and is printed on page 24.
5. Justin G. Schiller's article called "Annual Report of Librarian of Congress" which was printed on pp. 163–73 of a periodical called *AB Bookman's Weekly* on January 12, 1976.

POSSIBLE TOPICS FOR A RESEARCH PAPER

Almost any topic that interests you is fair game for research, but the two lists below may help you get started. The first list gives general topics that need to be limited and developed into theses. If those topics don't spark your interest, or if you can't see how to develop them into thesis statements, study the second list. It contains questions; an answer to any one of them could serve as your research paper's thesis.

A. GENERAL TOPICS

Alternatives to the Internal Combustion Engine
American Indians
Antiburglary Devices
Battle of Gettysburg
Beach Preservation
Diets
Endangered Animals
Health Foods
Indian Wars in Ohio
Islamic Movements

Literature
Marathons
Mass Transportation
Midwives
Nationalism in the Olympics
Prisons
Railroads
Religious Celebrations
Speech Disorders
Strip-Mining
Tax Reforms
U.S. Policies on Latin America
Vikings
Wilderness Preservation
Yoga

B. THESIS QUESTIONS

How did Ben Franklin's early reading affect his political ideas?
What are the origins of the fuel shortage?
Does television mean the end of imagination?
Why are this year's television programs so unsuccessful?
What is the attraction of science fiction?
Is automation a plague on American life?
What is the ideal family size?
How can we significantly improve the American school system?
What happens when small towns shrink?
Should newsmen have the right to protect their sources?
How can we be sure of high performance from our police?
Why haven't planned communities caught on in the U.S.?
Why do most Americans put loyalty to country above loyalty to
    state?
How have television and radio affected basic American freedoms?
Are dolphins more intelligent than man?
Is there anything to body language?
Why do many people believe in astrology?
How does the author of a book you have read develop the theme of
    the book?

section THREE

improving your punctu-ation and expression

PART VI
PUNCTUATION

By now you realize that there's much more to good writing than just getting all the commas and apostrophes in the right places, but those commas and apostrophes are also important. This part of the book begins with a brief chapter on grammar—but only what you need to know in order to learn the relatively few important rules of punctuation. The other chapters then teach punctuation.

We don't attempt to teach you all the rules of punctuation because, for example, you already know how to use a question mark and you don't need a colon or a dash very often. This part, then, teaches you only those common rules of punctuation we think you need to learn.

CHAPTER 23

Definitions

If you understand the terms in this chapter, learning to punctuate a sentence will be easy, for punctuation is not really very mysterious. In fact, once you understand these terms, you will probably be surprised just how easy punctuation can be. The catch (and, of course, there is a catch) is that you must work hard to understand them. Skimming this chapter once, or even reading it once through carefully, will not suffice. You have to (gasp!) memorize a few terms. So learn this material well, because all of it is essential in later chapters.

1. **Clause**—*A clause is a group of words containing a subject (S) and a verb (V).*

                  S   V
Clause: Robert climbed Pikes Peak.

Sometimes people are fooled into believing a group of words is a clause simply because it contains something that looks like a verb:

    Not a clause: Running along the beach.

The above group of words cannot be a clause for two reasons: (1) it has no subject; (2) it has no verb. Words that end in *-ing* and seem like verbs are really *verbals.* Just remember that an *-ing* word can never function by itself as a verb, and you will stay out of trouble. To be a verb, the *-ing* word must have a helper:

        S   V
Rosemary is running along the beach. (The word *is* is a helping verb.)

Because we have added a subject and a helping verb to the *-ing* word, we now have a clause.

    Clauses are either *independent* or *dependent.*

2. **Independent Clause (IC)**—*An independent clause is a clause that*

makes a complete statement and therefore may stand alone as a sentence.

                                      S   V

Independent Clauses: The monkey is brown.

                                         S   V

                                 The automobile runs smoothly.

                                      S   V

                                 Marilyn knows her.

                                    S   V

                                 (You) Close the door.

3.   Dependent Clause (DC)—*A dependent clause is a clause that makes an incomplete statement and therefore may not stand alone as a sentence.*

                                        S   V

Dependent Clauses: *Although* the monkey is brown...

                                  S   V

                                 If the automobile runs   smoothly...

                                        S   V

                                 ...*whom* Marilyn knows.

                                  S   V

                                 After you close the door...

Notice that a dependent clause is not a sentence by itself. That is why it is dependent—it depends on an independent clause in order to make a complete, or even an intelligible, statement. By itself, a dependent clause does not make any sense.

This definition and the one above on independent clause—though fairly standard, of course—may not satisfy you. Fortunately, we can offer another definition that works almost all the time (and the exceptions you don't need to worry about). A *dependent clause* almost always contains a subordinating conjunction or a relative pronoun (both covered later in this chapter; we've italicized them in the examples of dependent clauses above so you can see where they are). The subordinating conjunctions and relative pronouns are like red flags signaling dependent clauses. You can recognize an *independent clause,* then, because it's a clause not containing a subordinating conjunction or a relative pronoun.

4.   Sentence—*A sentence is a group of words containing at least one independent clause.*

Sentences (independent clauses are underlined once):

<u>Marilyn knows her</u>.

Although Marilyn knows her, <u>she does not know Marilyn</u>.

After you close the door, <u>Susan will turn on the record player</u>, and
<u>Sally will get the potato chips</u>.

5. Phrase (P)—*A phrase is a group of two or more related words not
containing both a subject and a verb.*

> Phrases: in the submarine
>
> running along the beach (remember, *-ing* words are not
> verbs)

6. Subordinating Conjunction (SC)—*A subordinating conjunction is a
kind of word that begins a* dependent *clause.*   You should memorize
the italicized words in the list of subordinating conjunctions below:

after	how	though
although	*if*	unless
as	in order that	until
as if	inasmuch as	*when*
as long as	provided	whenever
as much as	provided that	where
as though	*since*	wherever
because	so that	while
before	than	whether

Here are some examples of subordinating conjunctions beginning dependent clauses (the dependent clauses are underlined twice):

> SC
> Provided that your horse is properly registered, it may run in the
>
> race.
>
>   SC
> The race will be canceled if the rain falls.
>
>   SC
> Sign up for the trip to Memphis while vacancies still exist.

7. Relative Pronoun (RP)—*A relative pronoun is a kind of word that
marks a* dependent *clause.*   However, unlike a subordinating conjunc-

tion, it does not always come at the beginning of the dependent clause, although it usually does. You should memorize these five common relative pronouns:

who, whose, whom, which, that

Here are some examples of relative pronouns used in dependent clauses (the dependent clauses are underlined twice):

        RP
The lady who runs the beauty parlor is registering her horse.

        RP
The lady whose car lights are on is in the grocery store.

        RP
The lady whom I met is in the grocery store.

        RP
The schedule with which I was familiar is now obsolete.

        RP
The schedule that I knew is now obsolete.

Sometimes, unfortunately, these same five words can function as other kinds of words than relative pronouns, in which case they *do not* mark dependent clauses:

Not relative pronouns: Who is that masked man?

                        Whose golf club is this?

                        Whom do you wish to see?

                        Which car is yours?

                        That car is mine.

As a general rule, unless they are part of a question, the four words in our list that begin with *w* (*w*ho, *w*hose, *w*hom, and *w*hich) are relative pronouns. The other word, *that,* is trickier, but we can generally say that unless it is pointing out something, it is a relative pronoun. In the sentence "That car is mine," *that* points out a car, so it is not a relative pronoun.

8. Conjunctive Adverb (CA)—*A conjunctive adverb is a kind of word that marks an* independent *clause.*   Many students make punctuation

errors beca~~~~ ~~~~ subordinating conjunctions (which mark dependent ~~~~ ~~~~njunctive adverbs (which mark independent
clauses) ~~~~ ~~~~norize the italicized words in the list of conjunctive a~~~~

acc~~~~	hence	*nevertheless*
as a re~~~~	*however*	next
conseque~~~~	indeed	otherwise
first	in fact	second
for *example*	instead	still
for *instance*	likewise	*therefore*
furthermore	meanwhile	thus
	moreover	unfortunately

You may remember seeing some of these words before in the chapter
on coherence. A conjunctive adverb serves as a *transition,* showing the
relationship between the independent clause it is in and the independent
clause that preceded it.

A conjunctive adverb may not seem to mark an independent clause,
but it does. The following examples are perfectly correct as sentences because they are independent clauses:

CA
Therefore, I am the winner.

CA
However, the car is red.

Often a conjunctive adverb begins the second independent clause in a
sentence because that clause is closely related in meaning to the first independent clause:

CA
I finished in first place; therefore, I am the winner.

CA
You thought your new car would be blue; however, the car is
metallic brown.

Sometimes a conjunctive adverb will appear in the middle or even at the
end of a clause (that clause, of course, is still independent):

CA
I finished in first place; I am, therefore, the winner.

CA
I finished in first place; I am the winner, therefore.

9. Coordinating Conjunction (CC)—*A coordinating conjunction is a word that joins two or more units which are grammatically alike.* You should learn these seven coordinating conjunctions:

and, but, or, nor, for, so, yet

A helpful learning aid is that the coordinating conjunctions are all two or three letters long.

A coordinating conjunction can do the following:

CC
Join two or more words: Billy and Mary

CC
Join two or more phrases: in the car and beside the horse

CC
Join two or more dependent clauses: after the dance was over but before the party began

Join two or more independent clauses: He won the Philadelphia
CC
marathon, for he had been practicing several months.

Remember: Unlike subordinating conjunctions, relative pronouns, and conjunctive adverbs, the coordinating conjunction is not a marker for either an independent clause or a dependent clause. It simply joins two or more like items.

EXERCISES

A. Define these terms:

1. Clause _____

_____

_____

2. Independent Clause _____

_____

_____

3. Dependent Clause _____

_____

_____

4. Sentence _____

_____

_____

5. Phrase _____

_____

_____

B. After reading this chapter, you should know seven subordinating conjunctions, five relative pronouns, seven conjunctive adverbs, and seven coordinating conjunctions. Without referring to the lists in the chapter, see how well you can do.

    1. Write seven subordinating conjunctions. _____

_____

    2. Write five relative pronouns. _____

_____

    3. Write seven conjunctive adverbs. _____

_____

    4. Write seven coordinating conjunctions. _____

_____

C. 1. What two kinds of words mark dependent clauses? _____

_____

    2. What kind of word may mark an independent clause (an independent clause, of course, does not necessarily have a marker)? _____

_____

    3. What kind of word joins two or more units that are grammatically alike? _____

D. 1. Write two closely related independent clauses, the second of which contains a conjunctive adverb, and label the conjunctive adverb (CA). _____

_____

_____

2. Write an independent clause not containing a conjunctive adverb. _____

_____

3. Write a dependent clause containing a subordinating conjunction and label the subordinating conjunction (SC). _____

_____

4. Write a dependent clause containing a relative pronoun and label the relative pronoun (RP). _____

_____

5. Write two words joined by a coordinating conjunction and label the coordinating conjunction (CC). _____

_____

6. Write two phrases joined by a coordinating conjunction and label the coordinating conjunction (CC). _____

_____

7. Write two dependent clauses joined by a coordinating conjunction and label the coordinating conjunction (CC). _____

_____

8. Write two independent clauses joined by a coordinating conjunction you have not yet used and label the coordinating conjunction (CC). _____

_____

E. In the sentences below, underline the independent clauses once and the dependent clauses twice. Then label all subordinating conjunctions (SC), relative pronouns (RP), conjunctive adverbs (CA), and coordinating conjunctions (CC).

    1. The tiger is pacing in the cage.
    2. The movie that you wanted to see is playing at the Bijou.
    3. I'll go to the movie with you if you wait until tomorrow.
    4. That dolphin has learned to catch plastic rings.
    5. The man who trained the dolphin taught her to jump through a hoop.
    6. I wanted to watch television last night; however, I decided to read after I saw the programs available.

7. What programs are on television tonight?

8. I wanted to buy a new stereo; however, I couldn't afford even a new record.

9. Please turn off the light.

10. My sister studied piano, and I learned to play the clarinet.

11. Although my cousin Herman wanted to play an accordion, he settled on a harmonica.

12. Herman bought a music stand and a case for his harmonica.

13. If you have finished dressing and if the rain has stopped, perhaps we can go for a walk.

14. Many Americans are familiar with the Mayan temples in Central America; far fewer, however, realize that similar temples existed in the southeastern United States.

15. Because the temples and mounds in the Lower Mississippi Valley were made of perishable materials, little remains of them today.

CHAPTER 24

Sentence Fragment

A sentence fragment is an error involving punctuation.

Sentence Fragment (Frag)—*A sentence fragment is a group of words punctuated like a sentence but not containing an independent clause.* Because a sentence must have at least one independent clause, a sentence fragment is just a piece of a sentence. Here are some examples of sentence fragment errors:

Sentence Fragments: Running along the beach.

Even though the movie won an Oscar.

See? These so-called sentences are really frauds: they begin with a capital letter and end with a period, but they don't contain an independent clause.

Usually a sentence fragment is very closely related to the sentence that preceded it. The two examples above might have appeared in the following contexts:

Sentence Fragments: I finally found that stray mutt. Running along the beach.

Marie absolutely refused to go to the theater. Even though the movie had won an Oscar.

To correct a sentence fragment, either connect it to an independent clause or add a subject and a verb to convert it to an independent clause.

Correct: I finally found that stray mutt running along the beach. (fragment connected to an independent clause)

OR

Correct: I finally found that stray mutt. He was running along the beach. (fragment converted to an independent clause)

Correct: Marie absolutely refused to go to the theater even though the movie had won an Oscar. (fragment connected to an independent clause)

OR

Correct: Marie absolutely refused to go to the theater. The movie had won an Oscar. (fragment converted to an independent clause)

A final note: Although sentence fragments are usually inappropriate, they are permissible at certain times. You will see many of them in advertisements, but practically none in very formal writing. If you look closely, though, you can find a few in this book. However, your instructor will probably ask you not to use sentence fragments because you are always correct not to use them and often incorrect when you do use them. All right?

EXERCISES

A. Define sentence fragment. _____

_____

B. Write four sentence fragments.

1. _____

2. _____

3. _____

4. _____

C. Underline any "sentence" below that is only a fragment:

1. Sharon, a promising young actress.

2. You're right.

3. Yesterday Juan, who claimed he could master any video game, having taken on the challenge of winning at Pac-Man and losing.

4. Marianne, a rookie police officer, leaving the station house.

5. Teepees, usually made with animal hides on the plains, were made of bark in the woodlands.

6. After typing on a word processor for hours, Martha, worrying about whether the paper would be ready on time.

7. Perhaps so.

8. Every vacation when I visit my parents near the ocean, whether in the summer or the winter, fishing in the surf or pulling a net to catch shrimp for supper, but never going to eat in a seafood restaurant.

9. The crab legs were delicious. And the shrimp, as well.

10. Here today, gone tomorrow.

D. Correct the following sentence fragments.

1. Today movies frequently become television series. Because the story lines already have proved popular.

_____

_____

2. In Europe and in Asia the people were always friendly. No matter how little money we spent.

_____

_____

3. Dogs bark for several reasons. One major reason being to warn strangers away from their territory.

_____

_____

4. The setting for two major battles of the Civil War was near Manassas, Virginia. Located only a few miles outside Washington, D.C.

_____

_____

CHAPTER 25

Comma Splice and Fused Sentence

Comma splices and fused sentences are sentences that are punctuated incorrectly.

1. Comma Splice (CS)—*A comma splice occurs when two independent clauses are joined by only a comma.* In other words, it is two independent clauses "spliced" together with only a comma. Using the abbreviation IC for independent clause, we can express the comma splice as follows:

Comma splice: IC,IC.

Here are some comma splice errors:

Wrong: We hiked for three days, we were very tired.

Wrong: The television is too loud, the picture is fuzzy.

There are five ways to correct a comma splice:
a. Change the comma to a period and capitalize the next word. (IC. IC.)

Correct: We hiked for three days. We were very tired.

b. Change the comma to a semicolon. (IC;IC.)

Correct: We hiked for three days; we were very tired.

c. Change the comma to a semicolon and add a conjunctive adverb. (IC;CA,IC.)

Correct: We hiked for three days; hence, we were very tired.

d. Add a coordinating conjunction before the second independent clause. (IC,CC IC.)

Correct: We hiked for three days, so we were very tired.

e. Change one independent clause to a dependent clause. (DC,IC.)

Correct: Because we hiked for three days, we were very tired.

A very common form of comma splice occurs when only a comma precedes a conjunctive adverb at the beginning of the second independent clause in a sentence. (IC,CA,IC.)

Wrong: Mount Rainier is beautiful, however, it is also forbidding.

The best way to correct this kind of comma splice is to change the first comma to a semicolon.(IC;CA,IC.)

Correct: Mount Rainier is beautiful; however, it is also forbidding.

Another form of comma splice occurs when two independent clauses are separated by a dependent clause, but the strongest mark of punctuation is still only a comma. (IC,DC,IC.)

Wrong: The artist is selling the portrait, because he does not have enough money, he has run out of paint.

How would you correct the above sentence? Does the writer mean that the artist is selling the portrait because he does not have enough money? Or does the writer mean the artist has run out of paint because he does not have enough money? Here is one instance in which correct punctuation is important to meaning. One of several ways to correct the sentence is to place a period on the appropriate side of the dependent clause, depending on the meaning you wish to express. (IC DC. IC.) or (IC. DC,IC.)

Correct: The artist is selling the portrait because he does not have enough money. He has run out of paint.

Correct: The artist is selling the portrait. Because he does not have enough money, he has run out of paint.

2.   Fused Sentence (FS)—*A fused sentence occurs when two independent clauses are joined without punctuation or a coordinating conjunction.*   In other words, a fused sentence is a comma splice without the comma:

Fused Sentence:　IC IC.

Here are some fused sentence errors:

Wrong:　We hiked for three days we were very tired.

Wrong:　The television is too loud the picture is fuzzy.

Correct a fused sentence with essentially the same methods you used to correct a comma splice:
a. Add a period after the first independent clause and capitalize the next word: (IC. IC.)

Correct:　The television is too loud. The picture is fuzzy.

b. Add a semicolon after the first independent clause. (IC;IC.)

Correct:　The television is too loud; the picture is fuzzy.

c. Add a semicolon and a conjunctive adverb after the first independent clause. (IC;CA,IC.)

Correct:　The television is too loud; furthermore, the picture is fuzzy.

d. Add a comma and a coordinating conjunction after the first independent clause. (IC,CC IC.)

Correct:　The television is too loud, and the picture is fuzzy.

e. Change one independent clause to a dependent clause. (DC, IC.)

Correct:　Whenever the television is too loud, the picture is fuzzy.

EXERCISES

A. Define these terms.

1. Comma splice _____

_____

2. Fused sentence _____

_____

B. 1. Write a sentence that is a comma splice.

_____

2. Correct it five different ways.

a. _____

b. _____

c. _____

d. _____

e. _____

C. 1. Write a sentence that is a fused sentence.

_____

2. Correct it five different ways.

a. _____

b. _____

c. _____

d. _____

e. _____

D. In the blank before each sentence, write *CS* if the sentence has a comma splice, *FS* if it is a fused sentence, and *Correct* if it is correct.

_____ **1.** The book was good; unfortunately, I was sleepy.

_____ **2.** Even though the story was supposed to be a thriller, I couldn't stay awake.

_____ **3.** The water level in the creek is getting higher the tide must be coming in.

_____ **4.** The cat taunted the dog through the sliding glass door, the dog ran at her and hit the door.

_____ **5.** The tow truck driver started the winch, and the front of the car began to rise.

_____ **6.** The potter used coils to form the base of the vase, however, she formed the sides from thin slabs of clay.

_____ **7.** The play became a film the film's director changed the plot.

_____ **8.** When we looked for conch shells on the beach, we found that the surf had broken all of them.

_____ 9. In three hours we netted only two pounds of shrimp, because the shrimp were quite small, we used them for shrimp salad.

_____ 10. The motorcycle started with a roar, the rider drove off into the darkness.

_____ 11. The mouse was very small, but Helen was very frightened.

_____ 12. The room was cold the furnace was off all night.

_____ 13. The air express company will fly the package from Chicago to New York overnight; moreover, the company will deliver the package to your office tomorrow morning.

_____ 14. The waves lapped at the hull of the boat, the fishing line dangled limply over the water.

_____ 15. After the video recorder rewinds, we can watch the beginning of the movie again.

CHAPTER 26

Comma

This chapter presents the seven most important uses of the comma (,).
 1. *Use a comma after every item in a series except the last item.*

   Example: The three wrecked cars are maroon, purple, and orange.

You probably already knew to put a comma after the first item (*maroon*, in this case), but why do you need one after the next-to-last item (*purple*)? Consider this example:

   Example: The three wrecked cars are maroon, purple and orange, and beige.

   Commas tell your readers that you are moving to the next item in a series. When you omit a comma, you're telling them you're still in that same item—a compound item—so they won't have to reread your sentence.
 2. *Use a comma before a coordinating conjunction that joins two independent clauses. (IC,CC IC.)*

  IC   CC   IC

Examples: The roof always leaked, but he never bothered to fix it.

  IC   CC   IC

The rain bucket was dented, and the handle was broken.

Note: Do not confuse a coordinating conjunction that joins two verbs with a coordinating conjunction that joins two independent clauses:

  S   V   CC   V
The coffee table was scratched and covered with dust.

The coordinating conjunction above is not preceded by a comma because it connects only the two verbs *scratched* and *covered*.

3. *Use a comma after a dependent clause that begins a sentence.*
(DC,IC.)

	DC	IC

Examples: Although the house plants were healthy, he had never watered them.

	DC	IC

Because the coffee table was scratched, I refused to buy it.

4. *Use a comma after a long phrase that begins a sentence.* (Long Phrase, IC.) The word *long* is rather vague, of course, but usually you will wish to place a comma after an introductory phrase of three or more words.

	Long Phrase

Examples: Above the row of mountains, the clouds seemed motionless.

Long Phrase

Walking along the beach, Mary found a sand dollar.

5. *Use commas to set off any word, phrase, or clause that interrupts the flow of the sentence.* In other words, if you could set off a word or group of words with parentheses but do not wish to, then set off that word or group of words with commas.

Examples: The tramp, forlorn, lay sprawled in the alley.

Judy, together with Carrie, looked eagerly at the stack of envelopes.

Mary, who was strolling along the beach, found a sand dollar.

John Wilkes Booth assassinated Abraham Lincoln, President during the Civil War.

Notice that interrupters in the middle of sentences have commas on *both* sides.

6. *Use commas to set off nonrestrictive clauses.* This rule is actually an expansion of Rule 5, because all nonrestrictive clauses are interrupters. You may wonder, though, just what restrictive and nonrestrictive clauses are.

A *restrictive clause* is essential to defining whatever it modifies. In the following example, let's assume you have several brothers:

> My brother *who is wearing a red motorcycle helmet* is meaner than I am.

The restrictive clause ("who is wearing a red motorcycle helmet") is essential because it tells us which of your several brothers is meaner than you are. It *restricts* the word *brother* from any one of your brothers to the one wearing the helmet. If you left out the restrictive clause, we would not know which brother you meant. You probably noticed that these restrictive clauses are not interrupters and, therefore, are not set off with commas.

A *nonrestrictive clause* is not essential in defining whatever it modifies. Since it is not essential, you could omit it and everybody would still know who (or what) you are talking about. Now let's assume that you have only one brother:

> My brother, *who is wearing a red motorcycle helmet,* is meaner than I am.

Because you have only one brother, you could omit the nonrestrictive clause and still make sense. The word modified—"brother"—is not *limited* in any way by the clause; it is only described in more detail. In other words, without the clause we still know which brother you're talking about. Set off these nonrestrictive clauses with commas.

7. *Use a comma after a conjunctive adverb unless it is the last word in the sentence.* (CA,IC.) or (IC;CA,IC.) This rule applies no matter where the conjunctive adverb appears within the sentence.

Examples:

```
              IC                         CA
    ┌──────────────────────────┐    ┌─────────────
    I rescued the fair young damsel. However, the dragon
              IC
    ┌──────────────────┐
    singed my sword.
```

```
              IC                         CA
    ┌──────────────────────────┐    ┌─────────────
    I rescued the fair young damsel; however, the dragon
              IC
    ┌──────────────────┐
    singed my sword.
```

```
              IC                              IC
    ┌──────────────────────────────┐┌──────────────────
                                              CA
    I rescued the fair young damsel; the dragon, however,
    ┌──────────────────┐
    singed my sword.
```

Note: If, as in the last example, the conjunctive adverb is in the middle of the independent clause, it will have commas on *both* sides of it.

EXERCISES

A. Write the seven important rules for using a comma:

1. _____

_____

2. _____

_____

3. _____

_____

4. _____

_____

5. _____

_____

6. _____

_____

7. _____

B. Write a sentence illustrating each of the above rules:

1. _____

_____

2. _____

_____

3. _____

_____

4. _____

_____

5. _____

_____

6. _____

_____

7. _____

_____

C. In the following sentences, add commas where necessary:

1. The door to the bank manager's office was closed and the teller was too timid to knock.
2. Consequently no one would approve my out-of-state check.
3. The Navajo rug was too expensive yet I really wanted to buy it.
4. Bonzo a monkey in a film has become famous because of his costar.
5. The children were wide awake but their teacher couldn't raise her head from her desk.
6. The rain pelted the roof of the house and dripped through cracks in the shingles into the attic.
7. I remember all the figures in the telephone number; unfortunately I can't remember what order they go in.
8. The pastry chef who has a slight Swedish accent created that magnificent dessert. (Note: There is only one pastry chef.)
9. The pastry chef who has a slight Swedish accent created that magnificent dessert. (Note: There are several pastry chefs.)
10. After I complete this exercise I'm going out for a hamburger.
11. Running along the hall and stopping suddenly the cat flew across the slick linoleum.
12. No matter how hard I stared at the clock the minute hand never seemed to move.
13. As the sun rose high over the zoo the giraffes strolled through their grounds; the camel however only stood in the shade.
14. The waiter who has a large gravy stain on his shirt dropped a soup bowl near table four. (Note: There are several waiters.)
15. The waiter who has a large gravy stain on his shirt dropped a soup bowl near table four. (Note: There is only one waiter.)
16. The rain drumming against the west side of the house tapped gently on the window where I sat reading.
17. Carol seasoned the soup stock with a bouquet garni salt and pepper and celery seed.
18. Tonita didn't exhibit her statue because the janitor chipped it with the handle of his broom.
19. The cobra regretably is loose somewhere in the next room.
20. Before we reached the lodge snow was falling heavily and beginning to build up on the road.

CHAPTER 27

Semicolon

The semicolon (;) is stronger than a comma but weaker than a period. This chapter presents the two most important uses of the semicolon.

1. *Use a semicolon between two independent clauses closely related in meaning but not joined by a coordinating conjunction.* (IC;IC.)

Examples:
        IC   IC
Lee won some battles; Grant won the war.

               IC   IC
The pale sun rose over the frozen land; the arctic fox gazed quietly at the sky.

2. *Use a semicolon between two independent clauses when the second independent clause is joined to the first with a conjunctive adverb.* (IC;CA,IC.)

Examples:
                       IC
The Grand Canyon was one of the first national parks;
     CA   IC
however, it is still one of the most spectacular.

                      IC
Most former mining towns in the Rockies are now de-
         CA   IC
serted; unfortunately, many have been vandalized.

Note: If a conjunctive adverb is moved from the beginning of the second independent clause into the middle of it, the conjunctive adverb is then preceded by a comma instead of a semicolon; the semicolon, however, remains between the independent clauses.

Examples:
                      IC
The Grand Canyon was one of the first national parks;
                   IC
         CA
it is still, however, one of the most spectacular.

EXERCISES

A. Write the two important rules for using the semicolon:

1. _____

   _____

2. _____

   _____

B. Write a sentence illustrating each of the above rules:

1. _____

   _____

2. _____

   _____

C. In the following sentences, add semicolons and commas where necessary:

   1. Burial mounds provide scientists with artifacts of lost cultures unfortunately too often treasure hunters find the mounds first.

   2. When the zoo keeper fed the lion the tiger began to roar at the same time the leopard began to pace in its cage.

   3. After I lose five more pounds I'm going to celebrate with a large pizza with everything but anchovies.

   4. If you find an unbroken conch shell save it for me leave the oyster shells on the beach however.

   5. Nellie attended the auction to look for a small table however she didn't buy anything because the bidding was too high.

   6. The auctioneer began the bidding at fifty dollars the bidding quickly rose to one hundred.

   7. One type of Indian wampum was made of disc-shaped pieces of clam shells threaded on a string some necklaces today look like that early wampum.

   8. Although wampum served as a kind of money it may have originated as a kind of jewelry therefore the similarity of modern jewelry to Indian wampum is even more ironic.

   9. The Spanish conquistadors killed only small numbers of Indians when they conquered Central and South America the diseases the Spaniards brought ravaged the societies.

   10. Because the ancient settlers of the Americas crossed the Bering Strait early migrations were from north to south nevertheless in later years some cultural developments spread from groups in Central America to tribes in North America.

CHAPTER 28

Apostrophe

The apostrophe (') is, for very good reason, one of the most neglected marks of punctuation. Unlike the other punctuation marks, the apostrophe can usually be omitted without any loss of meaning. Because it is still an accepted convention of our language, however, we should know its two important uses.

1. *Use an apostrophe to show possession.*

> Examples: Bill's brown car
>
> the dog's fleas

Note A: To form the possessive, follow these general rules:
(1) If the word does not end in an *s*, add an apostrophe and an *s*:

> Base word: rose
> Possessive: rose's fragrance

(2) If the word does end in *s*, add only an apostrophe:

> Base word: dolls
> Possessive: three dolls' dresses

Notice that if the word is singular, you simply apply these rules. If the word is to be plural, however you make the word plural first, and then apply the rules.

> Examples: dog (singular)
> a dog's fleas (singular possessive)
> two dogs (plural)
> two dogs' fleas (plural possessive)

Note B: Some words—particularly those expressing units of time —may not seem possessive but still require an apostrophe:

> Examples: a day's work
> seven minutes' delay
> a month's pay

Note C: Do not use an apostrophe to show possession for personal pronouns (*yours, his, hers, its, ours, theirs*).

Wrong: it's shell is broken.
Correct: Its shell is broken.

2. *Use an apostrophe to show that letters have been left out of a word.*

Examples: *cannot* becomes *can't*
do not becomes *don't*
does not becomes *doesn't*
I will becomes *I'll*
let us becomes *let's*
it is becomes *it's*

Note: The word *it's*, by the way, has only two meanings: "it is" or "it has."

EXERCISES

A. Write the two important rules for using an apostrophe:

1. _____

_____

2. _____

_____

B. Write an example that illustrates each of the above rules:

1. _____

2. _____

C. What class of words does not use an apostrophe to show possession?

_____

D. Form the singular and plural possessive of these words:

	singular possessive	*plural possessive*
girl	_____	_____
typewriter	_____	_____
pencil	_____	_____
table	_____	_____
year	_____	_____
sheep	_____	_____
woman	_____	_____
baby	_____	_____
hour	_____	_____
bus	_____	_____

E. Add necessary apostrophes to these sentences:

1. Kristinas shoes are missing, but Jenifer found hers.
2. When both girls shoes are found, lets go to dinner.
3. The automobiles continued to pass down Ramons street.
4. Are the boys horses saddled yet?
5. Seven weeks delay is too much when the company was served notice three weeks early.
6. Dont you think its time you gave the dog its bath?
7. I cant see why Lins mother wont let her go.
8. Didnt you say that its no longer yours?
9. The shoplifter tried to leave the store with three pairs of childrens socks, one mans belt, and seven womens coin purses.
10. If you dont want Walters business, its all right with me.

CHAPTER 29

Quotation Marks

This chapter presents the two important uses of quotation marks (" ") and three rules for using other punctuation with quotation marks.

1. *Use quotation marks to enclose the exact words written or spoken by someone else.*

> Example: Irving Knoke stated, "If someone is looking for an easy way to commit suicide, all he needs to do is stick his thumb out on any road."

2. *Use quotation marks to enclose the title of a poem, short story, magazine article, or newspaper article.* In other words, use quotation marks to enclose the title of a work that is published as part of another work. Poems and short stories are rarely published separately; rather, they are usually part of a book that includes other poems or stories. Similarly, magazine articles appear as part of a magazine, and newspaper articles appear as part of a newspaper.

Note: The book, magazine, or newspaper title—that is, the title of the larger work containing the poem, short story, or article—should be underlined (or italicized).

> Example: "The Lottery," *Learning Fiction* (a short story in a collection of fiction)
>
> "The Love Song of J. Alfred Prufrock," *Poetry for First Graders* (a poem in a collection of poetry)
>
> "Why Your Husband Will Leave You," *Ladies Weekly Journal* (an article in a magazine)
>
> "Muhammad Ali Wins Again," *Cripple Creek News* (an article in a newspaper)

The following rules explain how to use other punctuation with quotation marks:

1. *Always place periods and commas inside quotation marks.*

Examples: I enjoyed reading "The Lottery."

I just read "The Lottery," a strange story by Shirley Jackson.

2. *Always place semicolons and colons outside quotation marks.*

Examples: I just read "The Lottery"; it is weird.

There are three really interesting characters in "The Lottery": Mrs. Hutchinson, Old Man Warner, and Mr. Summers.

3. A. *Place question marks and exclamation points inside quotation marks if the quotation is a question or an exclamation.*

Examples: The umpire yelled, "You're out!"

The coach asked politely, "Was Bench really out?"

Note: This rule applies even if the sentence is also a question or an exclamation.

Example: Was the coach polite when he asked the umpire, "Was Bench really out?"

B. *Place question marks and exclamation points outside quotation marks if the sentence is a question or an exclamation but the quotation is not.*

Examples: Who just said, "The ski lift is open"?
I can't believe he said, "The door is locked"!

EXERCISES

A. What are the two important uses of quotation marks?

1. _____

_____

2. _____

_____

_____

B.   1. What two marks of punctuation should you always place inside quotation marks? _____

_____

2. What two marks of punctuation should you always place outside quotation marks? _____

_____

3. When are question marks and exclamation points placed inside quotation marks? _____

_____

4. When are question marks and exclamation points placed outside quotation marks? _____

_____

C.   Add necessary quotation marks in these sentences. Be careful to
place quotation marks clearly inside or outside any other punctuation.

1. In Stephen Crane's short story The Blue Hotel , the Swede
says, Oh, I see you are all against me .
2. The Swede then screams, I don't want to fight !
3. Was he crazy when he said, Oh, I see you are all against me ?
4. Was he cowardly to scream, I don't want to fight ! ?
5. I read some interesting criticism of The Blue Hotel in the article The True Color of the Swede in *Perceptions of Fiction.*
6. My favorite detective stories are The Purloined Letter , Endless Night , and The Nine Mile Walk .
7. Besides The Purloined Letter , Edgar Allen Poe wrote two
other detective stories: The Murders in the Rue Morgue and The
Mystery of Marie Rogêt .
8. Did you know that an orangutang is the criminal in The Murders in the Rue Morgue ?
9. Would you rather read a detective story such as The Nine Mile
Walk or a poem such as Dover Beach ?
10. Literary critic Edmund Wilson made clear his feelings about
detective stories when he said this: there is no need to bore ourselves with this rubbish .

CHAPTER 30

Subordination

You probably know what *in*subordination is, but subordination is something else altogether.

When you first learned to read and write, almost every sentence was an independent clause: "Jane, see Spot." Every idea—small as it was— had exactly the same emphasis as every other idea. Of course, nobody in college writes like that, but too often college students have not progressed far enough from that grade-school style.

Your challenge is to combine related ideas into one sentence, giving them just the right emphasis. To succeed, you must learn subordination. We all know that a subordinate is someone who ranks lower than someone else. English has a rank structure, too:

> **Independent Clause**   more important
> **Dependent Clause**
> **Phrase**
> **Word**   less important

Ideas expressed in an independent clause naturally seem more important than ideas expressed by only a word. Subordination, then, reduces the emphasis of an idea by lowering its position on the rank structure. We might subordinate an idea originally in an independent clause by placing it in a dependent clause, a phrase, or—sometimes—even a word. For example:

>   IC   IC
> Original: Art flew to Gila Bend. He arrived on time.

> Subordination (a   DC   IC
> dependent clause): Because he flew to Gila Bend, Art arrived on time.

> Subordination   Phrase   IC
> (a phrase):   By flying to Gila Bend, Art arrived on time.

Notice that subordination here has two effects. First, it shows that Art's arriving on time (expressed above in the independent clause) is the important idea to the writer. Second, it shows the relationship between the two ideas: the words *because* in the first revision and *by* in the second revision act as road signs, telling the reader to be ready for a cause-effect relationship ("Because something happened, something else resulted." "Because he flew to Gila Bend, Art arrived on time.") These road signs make the reader's task much easier.

Now let's return to the example. We could have subordinated the second independent clause, instead, if we had decided that Art's flying to Gila Bend was more important than the idea that he arrived on time:

IC   IC

Original: Art flew to Gila Bend. He arrived on time.

Subordination (a   IC   DC
dependent clause): Art flew to Gila Bend, where he arrived on time.

Subordination   IC   Phrase
(a phrase):   Art flew to Gila Bend, arriving on time.

When you edit your own writing, therefore, you have to decide which ideas you wish to emphasize and which you wish to subordinate.

"But," you might protest, "I use subordination all the time." Sure you do—though probably not enough. Let's express some ideas in grade-school style, early college style, and a more sophisticated style:

Grade-school style: The girl is playing tennis.
Her name is Sally.
She is a beginner.
She is taking lessons.
Karen is teaching her.
Karen is a professional.
Karen teaches at the Andromeda Club.
Karen teaches every Tuesday morning.

Early college style: Sally is playing tennis.
She is taking beginning lessons from Karen.
Karen is a professional, and she teaches at the Andromeda Club every Tuesday morning.

Improved style: Sally is taking beginning tennis lessons from Karen, a professional who teaches at the Andromeda Club every Tuesday morning.

This last revision certainly is easier to read than either of the other versions. Why? Subordination pushes the unimportant ideas to the side of the stage so the viewer can easily see the star, the independent clause.

Here's a final tip to help you with subordination. On a first draft, you're naturally too busy thinking of ideas to worry about the best way to piece them together. After you finish that draft, though, take another trip through your paper—beginning to end—just working on the best way to combine your ideas into better sentences.

Remember, your work while you write makes your reader's work much easier. Subordination lets him see which ideas you consider important. And, after you finish school, that's the main reason you will write.

EXERCISES

A. Combine these simple sentences two different ways, emphasizing a different idea each time:

1. The Grand Canyon is in Arizona. It is especially beautiful at sunrise and sunset.

    a. _____

    b. _____

2. The tango is a fancy ballroom dance. Rudolph Valentino made it famous in the 1920's.

    a. _____

    b. _____

3. Richard Cory was an aristocrat. He was rich and envied.

    a. _____

    b. _____

4. The loon has a haunting call. It generally lives near wilderness lakes.

    a. _____

    b. _____

5. Guadaloupe is a Caribbean island. It is a French possession.

    a. _____

    b. _____

B. For each exercise below, combine all the simple sentences into one good sentence:

1. Sir Launcelot rode into the battle.
   He rode quickly.
   He captured twenty-seven enemy knights.
   He captured fourteen horses.
   He captured a mule.

   _____

   _____

2. The man was a con man.
   He looked like a real doctor.
   He wore a white coat.
   He wore a stethoscope.
   He spoke to the committee.
   He spoke convincingly.
   He spoke about the advantages of Thanatopsis Snake Oil.

   _____

   _____

3. Chen finally reached the mall.
   The mall is near the new baseball stadium.
   He rode buses for three hours.
   He transferred from one bus to another two times.
   He is exhausted.
   He is frustrated.
   He is starved.

   _____

   _____

   _____

CHAPTER 31

Sentence Variety

After reading the preceding chapter, you may suspect that "good" writing consists of one complicated sentence after another. Not so; you'd lose the reader after a couple of pages. On the other hand, how would you like to read sentence after sentence in grade-school or early college style? You may think the solution is to write all medium-length sentences, but really good writing consists of a mixture, both of *sentence lengths* and *sentence structures*.

SENTENCE LENGTH

Actually, not very many people have poor sentence variety from writing only long sentences. The problem is usually a series of short sentences:

> The new governor was sworn in today. He is a Democrat. Ten thousand people attended the ceremony. The governor gave a brief inaugural address. The governor promised to end unemployment. He said he would reduce inflation. He also promised to improve the environment. The audience gave him a standing ovation.

Pretty dismal, right? The average sentence length is only six and a quarter words, and all the sentences except the second are either six or seven words long—not overwhelming variety. Let's use the technique of subordination we learned in the last chapter to come up with something better:

> The new Democratic governor was sworn in today. At a ceremony attended by ten thousand people, he gave a brief inaugural address, promising to end unemployment, reduce inflation, and improve the environment. The audience gave him a standing ovation.

This version is certainly much easier to read, mainly because we've eliminated choppiness and subordinated some unimportant ideas. The average sentence is now thirteen words long, within the desirable goal of twelve to twenty words per sentence.

SENTENCE STRUCTURE

Let's look again at our bad example. Notice how many sentences begin with the subject (and its modifiers) of an independent clause:

> [The new governor] was sworn in today. [He] is a Democrat. [Ten thousand people] attended the ceremony. [The governor] gave a brief inaugural address. [The governor] promised to end unemployment. [He] said he would reduce inflation. [He] also promised to improve the environment. [The audience] gave him a standing ovation.

Every sentence begins with the subject of an independent clause. Surely there is a better way to move from sentence to sentence than to begin every one with the subject. Some should begin with dependent clauses, others with phrases, and still others with transitional words. For example, look again at the revision:

> The new Democratic governor was sworn in today. *At a ceremony attended by ten thousand people,* he gave a brief inaugural address, promising to end unemployment, reduce inflation, and improve the environment. The audience gave him a standing ovation.

The introductory phrases in the second sentence provide nice relief.

You may think *you* would never begin a lot of sentences the same way. Perhaps. However, during the first draft many writers think of an idea and then write it down: "Subject—verb"; they think of another idea and write it down: "Subject—verb"; and so on. Then, because they never revise that draft for sentence variety, their sentences all begin the same way. Check your last few papers to see if you have fallen into this bad habit.

Many sentences, of course, should begin with the subject of an independent clause; however, they should still not all look alike. They could end with a dependent clause, they could contain a couple of independent clauses, or they could contain a series of parallel phrases or clauses (see Chapter 32). The sentences in the paragraph you are now reading, for example, all begin with the subject of an independent clause, but after that beginning, their structures vary considerably.

SOME ADVICE

Good writing is not an automatic process, a flow of uninterrupted inspiration pouring forth from a ball-point pen. It is the result of a painstaking and very, very conscious process. If you want to write with good sentence variety, you have to check your draft to see if the variety is there. Don't just hope it will happen to you. After writing that draft, ask yourself these questions:

1. Are my sentences different lengths?
2. Do my sentences begin in a variety of ways?
3. Do those sentences that do begin with the subject of an independent clause have a variety of structures?

If your answers are "no," then edit your paper for sentence variety. Be careful, though, so you don't sacrifice clearness just for the sake of variety. And don't create grotesque, unnatural sentences. Variety is a means to achieve the goal of good writing—it is not the goal itself.

EXERCISES

Revise these paragraphs for better sentence variety. In both the original and your revision, circle the subject of the first independent clause in every sentence. Then compute the average number of words in each sentence (count all the words in the paragraph and divide by the number of sentences).

A. Original: Manufacturers of video games design them to be challenging. The manufacturers also design the games to be entertaining. This is true for games made for amusement arcades. It also applies to games made to be played on televisions at home. The games must challenge the player to insure sales. Often a player will drop five dollars or more in quarters into an arcade game. Another player might pay forty dollars for a game cartridge for television. No one will pay these prices unless the game offers a contest. That contest must last more than a few plays. At the same time, however, the games won't sell if they are too hard. Players have to feel they have a chance of winning. They won't buy if they don't feel they can win. Bright colors and lights add to the fun, of course. Still, the key to a game's being entertaining is the skill needed for average players. Those players should be able to develop the skill to play the game well. They should not be able to master it. The video games are like the chairs and beds in the Goldilocks story. The games can be neither too hard nor too soft.

Average number of words per sentence _____

Your revision: _____

_____

_____

_____

_____

_____

_____

_____

_____

_____

Average number of words per sentence _____

B. Original: Many people today associate Mickey Spillane only with television commercials for low-calorie beer. Paperback book racks reveal the real Spillane legacy. Mickey Spillane popularized a type of tough detective. For this detective ends justify means. Mike Hammer is the "hero" in Spillane's *I, the Jury*. Hammer seeks revenge for the brutal killing of a close friend. Hammer declares himself judge, jury, and executioner. Then Hammer breaks most ethical and social laws while he pursues his private brand of justice. Hammer's actions in other books are equally immoral. However, the ugliness always occurs as Hammer rights some wrong. For years the marketplace success of Spillane's books has been tremendous. *I, the Jury* was first published in 1947. Authors still routinely reproduce Mike Hammer and his ethic. The questionable honor of spawning modern paperback series belongs to Mickey Spillane. These series include the Avenger, the Revenger, and the Executioner. You are sure to find some of these wherever cheap literature is sold.

Average number of words per sentence _____

Your revision: _____

_____

_____

_____

_____

_____

_____

_____

_____

_____

_____

Average number of words per sentence _____

CHAPTER 32

Parallelism

Now that you've studied sentence variety, you may be afraid of writing sentences that repeat simple patterns. Don't be. Some ideas work best in sentences that clearly show a pattern. When you analyze an idea, you take pains to discover similarities and differences among its parts. Whether you intend to compare or contrast those elements, you want the reader to see how the parts are alike or different. Parallelism is the key.

The principle of parallel construction is simple: *be sure ideas that are similar in content and function look the same.* Parallelism works in a sentence because the similarity of the appearance of the items shows clearly the pattern of the thought. The principle of parallelism applies most often to two or more items in a series with a coordinating conjunction and to pairs of items with correlative conjunctions (explained below).

ITEMS IN A SERIES WITH A COORDINATING CONJUNCTION

The principle of parallelism requires that all items in a series must be grammatically alike. That is, all words in a series must be the same type of word, all phrases the same type of phrase, and all clauses the same type of clause. Two or more items in a series normally use a coordinating conjunction (CC): *and, but, or, nor, for, so,* or *yet.* Thus, the series looks like this:

> item, *CC* item

or this

> item, item, *CC* item.

Here are sentences with parallel constructions:

234

words in series:
$$\overset{\text{item CC item}}{\text{I saw }\boxed{\text{John}}\boxed{\text{and}}\boxed{\text{Mary}}.}$$

$$\overset{\text{item item CC item}}{\text{I saw }\boxed{\text{John,}}\boxed{\text{Bill,}}\boxed{\text{and}}\boxed{\text{Mary}}.}$$

phrases in series:
$$\overset{\text{item \qquad CC \qquad item}}{\text{I see him }\boxed{\text{going to work}}\boxed{\text{and}}\boxed{\text{coming home}}.}$$

$$\overset{\text{item \qquad\qquad CC \quad item}}{\text{I plan }\boxed{\text{to eat in a restaurant}}\boxed{\text{and}}\boxed{\text{to see a}}}$$
movie.

dependent clauses
in series:
$$\overset{\text{item}}{\text{The phone rang }\boxed{\text{when I reached the motel}}}$$
$$\overset{\text{CC \qquad\qquad item}}{\boxed{\text{but}}\boxed{\text{before I unpacked my suitcases}}.}$$

independent clauses
in series:
$$\overset{\text{item \qquad CC \qquad item}}{\boxed{\text{I liked the parrot,}}\boxed{\text{so}}\boxed{\text{I bought it for my}}}$$
mother.

Notice that each item—word, phrase, or clause—in a series has the same form as the other items in the same series.

Although words in a series seldom present special problems, if the words are preceded by the articles *a, an,* or *the,* be sure the articles fall in one of these two patterns:

article word, word, CC word

article word, *article* word, CC *article* word

Notice the placement of the articles in these sample sentences:

Wrong: I bought food for *the* dog, cat, and *the* horse.

Correct: I bought food for *the* dog, cat, and horse.

Correct: I bought food for *the* dog, *the* cat, and *the* horse.

The correct sentences have either an article before the entire series or an article before every item in the series.

Unlike words in a series, phrases often cause problems. Many times students mix types of phrases. Be sure that *-ing* phrases fit with other *-ing* phrases, *to* phrases with *to* phrases, and so forth.

Wrong: I like *swimming in the pond, cycling down the lane,* and *to ride horses in the pasture.*

Correct: I like *swimming in the pond, cycling down the lane,* and *riding horses in the pasture.*

Correct: I like *to swim in the pond, to cycle down the lane,* and *to ride horses in the pasture.*

Wrong: I plan *to study hard, doing well on my exams,* and *to graduate with honors.*

Correct: I plan *to study hard, to do well on my exams,* and *to graduate with honors.*

Correct: I plan on *studying hard, doing well on my exams,* and *graduating with honors.*

Clauses in a series seldom cause major problems. However, if the series contains dependent clauses, you can help your reader by signaling the beginning of each dependent clause. Consider this sentence:

I expect to be entertained if I'm going to pay three dollars to get in a theater and I'm going to sit there for two hours.

What does the *and* join? Does it join the two independent clauses?

Or does it join two dependent clauses?

The intended meaning is probably the second one: the *and* joins two dependent clauses. The reader will more easily see the separation of items if the writer repeats the word that signals the beginning of the clauses:

Now the meaning is clear. Here's another sample:

"I can see that you don't like the meal and that you'd rather not be here," she pouted.

Notice that the repetition of *that* (which signals the beginning of dependent clauses) makes the parallel construction clear.

In addition to having like words, like phrases, and like clauses in a series, be sure that the items in a series are the same type of grammatical unit. Do not, for instance, mix phrases and clauses in a series, as in this sentence:

item CC   item

Wrong: My roommate likes to sleep in bed and when he's in class.

The sentence is awkward because the writer has joined a phrase (*in bed*) with a clause (*when he's in class*). Here's what the writer should have written:

Correct: My roommate likes to sleep when he's in bed and when he's in class.

Now a clause fits with a clause. (Notice also that the sentence repeats *when*, the word that signals the beginning of each dependent clause.)

PAIRS OF ITEMS WITH CORRELATIVE CONJUNCTIONS

Correlative conjunctions mate pairs of related items. Common correlative conjunctions are these: *either... or; neither... nor; not (only)... but (also);* and *whether... or.* The rule for parallelism with correlative conjunctions is simple: the grammatical units following each of the correlative conjunctions must be alike. Items mated by correlative conjunctions (CorC) will look like this:

CorC item *CorC* item.

Here are sentences with such pairs:

CorC   item   CorC   item

I don't like either his appearance or his manners.

CorC item CorC   item

Neither my aunt nor my cousin will speak to me.

Can you find the problem in this sentence?

> Wrong: *Either* I go to bed early *or* get up late.

This sentence demonstrates the most common failure to maintain parallelism with correlative conjunctions: *either* precedes the subject of the sentence (*I*), but *or* precedes the second verb (*get*). There are two methods to deal with the problem:

> Correct: I *either* go to bed early *or* get up late.

> Correct: *Either* I go to bed early *or* I get up late.

The first solution moves *either* so that both correlative conjunctions precede verbs (*go* and *get*). The second solution places *either* and *or* before subjects of clauses (*I* and *I*). In both corrections, the grammatical units following each correlative conjunction are alike.

All of this may seem complicated, but it's not. You wouldn't try to compare apples and automobiles, because they're not alike. Similarly, you can't expect your reader to accept a comparison of items that don't appear to be alike. The principle of parallelism requires only that you make like items *look* alike so the reader can see the similarity.

EXERCISES

A.   1.   Name the seven coordinating conjunctions. _____

_____

2.   Explain the principle of parallelism as it applies to a series with a coordinating conjunction. _____

_____

3.   Name the four common pairs of correlative conjunctions.

_____

_____

4.   Explain the principle of parallelism as it applies to a pair of items with correlative conjunctions. _____

_____

B.   Improve the parallelism in each of the following sentences:

1.   I talked to a doctor, a salesman, and to a crane operator.

2. Flora likes to go to the playground to jump rope, to swing, and sliding.

3. I bought the towel, sheet, and the bedspread.

4. Having just arrived at the beach, Thea both wanted to sunbathe and to swim.

5. The coach can either complain to the official or he can keep quiet.

6. Ed loves backpacking, camping, and especially to climb mountains.

7. The lifeguard knew that the waves were high and they were dangerous.

8. José hooked a walleye, perch, and a trout.

9. Nathan enjoys swimming, cycling, and to ride horses.

10. At Christmas we like to decorate the tree, making special cookies, and singing carols.

11. Overcome by the paperwork and with the telephone ringing constantly, Stackley reached quickly for the aspirin.

12. Not only the students but also those who teach them were upset by the new university policy.

13. This summer Tony plans to lie in the sun, swim in the pool, and generally avoiding work.

14. The director wanted to film scenes in the jungles of the Philippines and where the streets were crowded in Manila.

15. Before going onto the stage and she heard the opening applause, Gayle was very nervous.

16. Rosa skipped the lecture because she didn't have the time, the energy, and wasn't interested.

17. I think about Grandmother's farm when I drive in rush-hour traffic or I read about crime in the streets.

18. I'll decide to go if it neither interferes with my other plans nor it comes too late in the day.

19. The fountain was beautiful as the droplets spread out in the air and were made to sparkle by the sunlight.

20. Carlos went to the party for the food, the entertainment, and to meet people who might become customers.

CHAPTER 33

Misused Modifiers

Dangling participle! Nothing—not even "split infinitive"—can strike such terror in the heart of an English student. But don't be afraid. Behind the fancy name is a simple concept you'll understand after studying this chapter. You won't learn the differences between dangling participles, dangling gerunds, and dangling infinitives because the differences aren't really important: we'll treat them all more simply as *dangling modifiers*. In addition to that special type of modifier problem, you'll also study *misplaced modifiers*. But first, you may wonder what a modifier is.

Modifiers are words, phrases, or clauses that limit or describe other words. For example, in "I never saw a purple cow," the modifier *purple* limits the discussion from "all cows" to only "purple cows."

As you've seen in earlier chapters, modifiers allow you to combine several ideas into one sentence. You might write this:

Jonathan ate the doughnut. It was the only doughnut.

However, you save time and space by reducing the second sentence to a modifier:

Jonathan ate the *only* doughnut.

Still, there is a catch: word order in an English sentence often determines meaning; therefore, different word arrangements may yield different meanings. Let's see what happens if we place *only* in every possible position in "Jonathan ate the doughnut."

Only Jonathan ate the doughnut.	(No one else ate it.)
Jonathan *only* ate the doughnut.	(He didn't do anything else to it.)
Jonathan ate *only* the doughnut.	(He ate nothing else.)

Jonathan ate the *only* dough-nut.	(There were no other dough-nuts.)
Jonathan ate the doughnut *only*.	(He ate nothing else.)

Five combinations yield four distinctly different meanings. Play this game with other sentences and words such as *only, almost, most, just, every, merely,* and *nearly*.

The game's implication is obvious: unless you carefully place the modifiers in your sentences, you may not write what you really mean. If modifiers do not clearly modify what they are supposed to, they may obscure your meaning, or they may make you look ridiculous.

MISPLACED MODIFIERS

Placing a modifier in a sentence requires good judgment and careful editing. No particular place in a sentence is always right for a modifier, but this much is true: a modifier tends to modify what it is close to. "Close to" may be before or after the thing modified, so long as the sentence makes sense. These sentences don't make much sense:

1. A jeep ran over the soldier *that had muddy tires.*
2. People stared in amazement *on the sidewalk.*
3. The accident left *neatly pressed* tire marks on the soldier's shirt.

In these sentences something comes between the modifiers and the things modified. As a result, the modifiers appear to refer to the things they are closest to: *that had muddy tires* seems to modify *soldier; on the sidewalk* seems to refer to *amazement;* and *neatly pressed* appears to modify *tire marks.*

Let's move the modifiers so that they modify what they should.

1. A jeep *that had muddy tires* ran over the soldier.
2. *On the sidewalk,* people stared in amazement.

OR

People *on the sidewalk* stared in amazement.

3. The accident left tire marks on the soldier's *neatly pressed* shirt.

Notice that *on the sidewalk* works before or after *people,* whereas *that had muddy tires* works only after *jeep* and *neatly pressed* works only before shirt. What matters, then, is that the modifier must be close enough to the thing it modifies to complete the thought logically.

A second type of placement problem occurs when you write strings of modifiers. Consider this example:

A man *with red hair in a green suit* crossed the street.

Both *with red hair* and *in a green suit* should modify *man,* but instead *in a green suit* seems to refer to *hair.* One solution is to put one modifier before and another after the thing modified:

A *red-haired* man *in a green suit* crossed the street.

OR

Wearing a green suit, a man *with red hair* crossed the street.

A second solution is to combine the modifiers with a coordinating conjunction:

A man *with red hair and a green suit* crossed the street.

Again, the exact position of the modifier doesn't matter if the result makes sense.

DANGLING MODIFIERS

Dangling modifiers can occur anywhere in a sentence, but the most common problem is at the beginning. A modifier that *begins* a sentence must refer to something that follows. Because of convention, readers expect an introductory word or phrase modifier to refer to the subject of the sentence.

Walking along the beach, Mary found a sand dollar.

Since we expect the opening phrase (*walking along the beach*) to modify the subject of the sentence (*Mary*), we know that Mary, not the sand dollar, was walking along the beach. But what if the sentence reads as follows?

Walking along the beach, a sand dollar was found by Mary.

Again we expect the introductory phrase to modify the subject of the sentence, but sand dollars don't walk. Since the modifier cannot logically modify the subject of the sentence, we say that the modifier "dangles."

The following sentences contain dangling modifiers:

1. *Enthusiastic,* the hour seemed to pass quickly.
2. *Finishing the game,* the crowd loudly booed the home team.

3. *After examining the data,* the steam engine appeared to be the best choice.
4. *To enjoy surfing,* the waves must be high.
5. *When only nine,* John's mother took him to a circus.

Was the hour enthusiastic? Did the crowd actually finish the game? Did the steam engine examine the data? Can waves enjoy surfing? Do you really believe that John had a mother who was only nine years old? Because the modifiers above have no logical connection to the subjects of the sentences, the modifiers dangle.

You have two options to correct dangling modifiers. The most obvious method is to rewrite the sentence so that the subject matches the modifier.

1. Enthusiastic, we thought the hour passed quickly.
2. Finishing the game, the home team heard loud booing from the crowd.
3. After examining the data, we concluded that the steam engine was the best choice.
4. To enjoy surfing, you need high waves.
5. When only nine, John went to a circus with his mother.

These corrections leave the modifier unchanged.

The second method is to change the phrase or word modifier into a clause.

1. Because we were enthusiastic, the hour seemed to pass quickly.
2. As the game ended, the crowd loudly booed the home team.
3. After we examined the data, the steam engine appeared to be the best choice.
4. If you want to enjoy surfing, the waves must be high.
5. When he was only nine, John's mother took him to a circus.

You can avoid problem modifiers—misplaced as well as dangling—if you keep in mind the essential relationship between modifiers and the things they refer to: a modifier tends to modify what it is close to, and a modifier should be close to what it must modify.

EXERCISES

A. 1. When is a modifier misplaced? _____
_____

2. How can you correct a misplaced modifier? _____

_____

3. When does a modifier dangle? _____

_____

4. How can you correct a dangling modifier? Name two ways.

   a. _____

   _____

   b. _____

   _____

B. 1. Write one sentence with a misplaced modifier and one with a dangling modifier.

   a. _____

   _____

   b. _____

   _____

2. Now correct your sentences.

   a. _____

   _____

   b. _____

   _____

C. Rewrite the following sentences to eliminate the modifier problems.

   1. Wearing the fur-lined coat, the sharp Chicago wind did not disturb Julio.
   2. The horse jumped the fence with its mane flying in the wind.
   3. Having reached the campsite, the tent was erected by the tired campers.
   4. Stretching far to the left to catch the badly thrown ball, the runner darted past the catcher at home plate.
   5. The cold policeman sipped the coffee with an expression of contentment.
   6. After reaching a rolling boil, the cook can skim the fat from the surface of the soup.

7. Bubbling with excitement, the ribbons and paper were torn from the package by the child.

8. A little girl holding a broken bottle with a cut on her knee sat crying on the curb.

9. A dog chewed the bone with brown and white patches.

10. To insure they arrive by Christmas, the cards should be mailed by 10 December.

11. A girl in a raincoat with a Girl Scout uniform was standing outside the supermarket selling cookies in the rain.

12. Scrambling over the ice, the bullet struck the polar bear.

13. Don't let him play in the snow with that lightweight coat on.

14. Dropping my shoe on the floor, the sound echoed loudly through the house.

15. When completely filled out and checked, the taxpayer should sign the form.

CHAPTER 34

Subject-Verb Agreement

You've learned in school that there are many rules in grammar, and you've probably learned from experience that the ways to make mistakes in grammar are more numerous than the rules. But you can apply most of the rules correctly already. This chapter deals with only one grammar problem—agreement between subjects and verbs. The rule itself is quite simple: *a verb must agree in number with its subject.* If the subject is singular, the verb must be singular; if the subject is plural, the verb must be plural.

Usually the verb itself doesn't cause trouble. In fact, the forms for many singular and plural verbs are identical, so you can't make a mistake in agreement. Yet English verbs retain one peculiarity that some students find troublesome. You know that an *-s* or *-es* ending on a noun makes the noun plural. The same would seem to be true for verbs, but it isn't. An *-s* or *-es* ending on a verb makes the verb singular:

Plural	*Singular*
They run.	He runs.
They go.	She goes.
They jump.	It jumps.

Other than this simple difference between verbs and nouns, the verb doesn't cause much difficulty. Most errors in agreement, then, occur because of some difficulty related to the subject. Some problems arise from trouble with *identifying the subject*; others result from uncertainty in *recognizing the subject's number.*

IDENTIFYING THE SUBJECT

We can usually find the subject if it comes in its ordinary place—just before the verb—but we may have trouble if it follows the verb. Watch for sentences opening with *there* or *here*. These words delay the subject so that it appears after the verb. You'll have to think through such a sentence because you won't know whether the verb should be singular or plural until you get beyond it to the subject.

        V   S
There *are* three *sailboats* at the dock.

        V   S
There *is* the *sailboat* with the sail on upside down.

     V   S
Here *are* the *supplies* you ordered.

     V   S
Here *is* the *box* you wanted first.

Sometimes even when the subject comes before the verb, it is still hard to identify, especially if we have written a phrase between the subject and the verb. Then we might think a word in that phrase is the subject or (just as bad) that the phrase is part of the subject and therefore makes it plural. Let's look first at an example in which a word in the phrase might seem to be the subject:

                    S   V
Wrong: One of the Coyne *boys have climbed* the water towe.

Here the word *boys* is so close to the verb that the writer thought it was the subject. He was wrong. *Boys* is simply part of a phrase that comes between the subject and the verb. The real subject is *one:*

          S   V
Correct: *One* of the Coyne boys *has climbed* the water tower.

Now let's look at a phrase that might seem to be part of the subject:

                    S   V
Wrong: *Martha, as well as her sisters, work* in the fields regularly.

As well as her sisters seems to be part of the subject. It seems to be equivalent to *and her sisters*. But it isn't. *As well as* and these other words below are merely prepositions and therefore have nothing to do with determining the agreement between a subject and its verb.

as well as	including
accompanied by	like
along with	together with
in addition to	with

How can we find the subject in our example above? Mentally eliminate the entire phrase:

                                    S   V
Correct: *Martha* (~~as well as her sisters~~) *works* in the fields reg-
           ularly.

The subject is now clear.

RECOGNIZING THE SUBJECT'S NUMBER

The problems we just looked at occur because the subject isn't where we expect it to be. Sometimes, though, we can find the subject and still not know whether it is singular or plural. These rules will help you:

1. Two or more subjects joined by *and* are almost always plural. The *and* joins the items—singular, plural, or mixed—into one plural unit.

         S   S   V
Charlotte and her *mother drive* the metallic brown dune buggy.

         S   S   V
That *woman* and her *husband look* a lot alike.

There is an exception: if the two subjects joined by *and* refer to a single person or act as a single unit, then use a singular verb.

         S   S   V
A *scholar* and *gentleman is* what we need for a leader.

2. If *or* or *nor* joins subjects, the verb agrees with whichever subject is closer to the verb.

         S   S   V
Either *Beverly* or my other *aunts have* my thanks.

Here *aunts* is closer to the verb than *Beverly*, so the verb is plural. What if we reverse the subjects?

                          S   S   V
Either my other *aunts* or *Beverly has* my thanks.

Now *Beverly* is closer, so the verb is singular.

This rule still applies if both items are singular or if both items are plural. If both are singular, naturally a singular subject will be next to the verb, so the verb is singular. Likewise, if both subjects are plural, a plural subject will be next to the verb, so the verb is plural.

3. *Some, all, none, part, half* (and other fractions) may be either singular or plural, depending on the phrase that follows them. You probably

think we're crazy because we told you in the first part of the chapter not to let a phrase between the subject and the verb influence subject-verb agreement. Well, here is an exception to that rule.

Many times the words in the list above are followed by a phrase beginning with *of* ("All *of* the jurors...," "Some *of* the tea..."). If the main word in the *of*-phrase is plural, then the verb should be plural. However, if the main word is singular or just can't be counted (we wouldn't say "one *milk*" or "thirteen *tea*," for example), then the verb should be singular.

S   V
Some of the grapes *are* still on the table. (*grapes* is plural, so the verb is plural)

S   V
Some of the milk *is* *dripping* on the floor. (*milk* cannot be counted, so the verb is singular)

4. Relative pronouns (*who, whose, whom, which,* and *that*) may be singular or plural, depending on the word they replace. Usually the relative pronoun replaces the word just before it:

S   V
Jeannette is one of the children *who* *love* to read. (*Who* is a pronoun replacing *children*. Not just one child but all the children love to read.)

Again, here comes an exception. What if Jeannette is the only one in the group who loves to read? Then the pronoun *who* replaces the word *one,* not the word *children:*

S   V
Jeannette is the only one of the children *who* *loves* to read.

The exception, then, is that in the phrase *the only one... who/that,* the relative pronoun refers to the word *one,* so the verb must be singular (after all, what can be more singular than *one?*).

EXERCISES

A. Use one of the following verbs when completing this exercise:
   singular verbs: throws, goes, misses, takes
   plural verbs: throw, go, miss, take
Do not use other forms of these verbs (such as *threw, had thrown,* or the like).

1. a. Write a sentence that has the subject following the verb. Use a singular verb.

_____

   b. Now use a plural verb.

_____

2. Write a sentence with a singular subject and the phrase "as well as (*fill in a word*)" between the subject and the verb.

_____

3. Write a sentence that has two subjects joined by *and.*

_____

4. a. Write a sentence with two plural subjects joined by *or.*

_____

   b. Write a sentence with two singular subjects joined by *or.*

_____

   c. Write a sentence with a singular and a plural subject joined by *or*.

_____

   d. Rewrite sentence *c* but reverse the order of the subjects.

_____

5. Write a sentence with *all* as the subject and a phrase beginning with *of* between it and the verb.

_____

6. Write a sentence that contains a relative pronoun as a subject and draw an arrow to its antecedent.

_____

B. Circle the correct verb.

   1. There (is, are) five apple trees on the closest hill.
   2. Laura, together with her friends, (is, are) playing Old Maid.
   3. That rabbit is the only one of the animals that (like, likes) the snow.
   4. All of the sugar (is, are) melted.
   5. One of the dogs or the cat (is, are) banging into the door.
   6. Brooke is the only one of the tennis players who (has, have) a chance.
   7. Everybody following the crowds and looking at the races on the lake this afternoon (is, are) well pleased.
   8. Do you think three desks and a table (is, are) enough?

9. Ed, accompanied by Jeannette, (is, are) going to Wrightsville Beach in July.

10. Some of the factory workers (is, are) ready to strike.

11. Some of the tea (is, are) too bitter to drink.

12. The star forward, along with the rest of his teammates, (was, were) flabbergasted by the referee's astounding call.

13. There (has, have) been fewer burglaries since the two starved Bengal tigers escaped.

14. The type of spark plug that the mechanics use in classic sports cars (is, are) unbelievably expensive.

15. Those books, including that first edition of an Evan Robinson classic, (is, are) worth more than you and I can imagine.

16. Jenny is the only one of the children who (like, likes) the licorice gumdrops.

17. Several lamps from the furniture shop (is, are) supposed to be packed for these customers.

18. Carmelita is one of the ladies who (is, are) sailing in the race.

19. Here (is, are) the two wrestlers who had trouble cutting weight for the meet.

20. Neither the champ nor his trainers (want, wants) him to go back into the ring.

CHAPTER 35

Pronoun Agreement

This chapter deals with another agreement problem—agreement between pronouns and the things they refer to.

Because pronouns replace nouns or other pronouns in sentences, a pronoun must have something to refer to (called the antecedent of the pronoun). Look for the antecedent for *his* in this sentence:

The boy found his dog.

Clearly, *his* refers to *boy*, so *boy* is the antecedent for *his*.

The grammar rule that students find troublesome is this: *a pronoun must agree in number with its antecedent.* If the antecedent is singular, the pronoun must be singular; if the antecedent is plural, the pronoun must be plural.

Because the pronoun's number depends on the antecedent, our attention should be on problem antecedents. When the antecedent is simple, making the pronoun agree is a simple task. You wouldn't write this:

The *boys* looked for *his* books. (Assume all the boys are missing books.)

Boys is a plural antecedent, so you'd write this:

The *boys* looked for *their* books.

Yet, special problems do arise with two types of antecedents: *indefinite pronoun antecedents* and *compound antecedents.*

INDEFINITE PRONOUN ANTECEDENTS

The biggest headache connected with pronoun agreement occurs when the antecedent is an indefinite pronoun like *everyone* or *nobody*. We needn't be concerned here with all indefinite pronouns, but we must look at one problem group.

The following indefinite pronouns are singular and always require singular pronoun references:

each	everyone	everybody
either	someone	somebody
neither	anyone	anybody
another	no one	nobody
one		

The words formed from *-one* (like *everyone*) and from *-body* (*everybody*) often seem to be plural, but they're not. Try thinking of them as if they had the word *single* in the middle, like this: *every-single-one* or *every-single-body*. Now they seem to be singular, as they really are.

An unusual mental block is associated with these indefinite pronouns. Few people would write this:

Everyone *have* a coat.

Have just doesn't sound right following *everyone*. And for good reason. *Have* is plural, but *everyone* is singular. Yet, often the same people who recognize *everyone* as a singular subject have trouble recognizing *everyone* as a singular antecedent. Far too often they write this:

Everyone *has their* coat.

Has, of course, is correct: the singular verb agrees with the singular subject. But plural *their* cannot refer to singular *everyone*. As illogical as this problem seems, it is still common.

Study these samples:

Wrong: Everyone wore *their* coat.

Correct: Everyone wore *his* coat.

Wrong: Nobody looked at *their* books.

Correct: Nobody looked at *his* books.

You may be uneasy with these correct answers because often the *everyone* you are talking about refers to a mixed group of men and women, in which case the word *his* may seem inappropriate. You're right, of course. We're sure the convention of using *his* will someday change. But for now —at least in writing—the change has not taken place.

By themselves, *each, either, neither, another,* and *one* seldom cause problems because they're obviously singular. Usually, however, these pronouns are followed by a phrase beginning with *of* and ending with a plural noun, like these:

> Each of the girls . . .
>
> Either of the students . . .

Don't be fooled. The singular indefinite pronoun, not the word in the *of*-phrase, is the antecedent for a pronoun in the rest of the sentence.

> Wrong: Each of the girls gave me *their* money.
>
> Correct: Each of the girls gave me *her* money.

The pronoun refers to *each,* not to *girls.*

> Wrong: Either of the students may bring *their* books.
>
> Correct: Either of the students may bring *his* books.

His refers to *either,* not to *students.*

COMPOUND ANTECEDENTS

Compound antecedents may be joined with *and, or,* or *nor.* And the antecedents themselves may be all singular, all plural, or a mixture of singular and plural. The rules for agreement depend on the various combinations of these factors.

1. Two or more antecedents joined by *and* require a plural pronoun. It makes no difference whether the antecedents are singular, plural, or mixed: the *and* makes the compound antecedent plural.

> John and the other boy found *their* seats.
>
> John and the other boys found *their* seats.

2. Plural antecedents joined by *or* or *nor* require a plural pronoun.

> Either the boys or the girls will clean *their* rooms first.
>
> Neither the boys nor the girls want to clean *their* rooms.

3. Singular pronouns joined by *or* or *nor* require a singular pronoun.

Either the dog or the cat will get *its* food first.

Neither the dog nor the cat will eat *its* food.

4. When *or* or *nor* joins a singular antecedent and a plural antecedent, the pronoun agrees with whichever antecedent it is closer to.

Neither Freddy nor the other boys like *their* jobs. (The pronoun *their* agrees with *boys*.)

Neither the other boys nor Freddy likes *his* job. (*His* agrees with Freddy.)

You may not like the second sample sentence here, even though it is technically correct. Many readers feel uncomfortable when the singular antecedent of a singular-plural set determines the number of the pronoun reference. It's a good idea, then, to place the plural antecedent closer to the pronoun reference so that the pronoun may be plural.

EXERCISES

A. Circle the correct pronoun in each set of choices below.

1. Neither Jennifer nor the other girls remembered (her, their) assignments.
2. Each of the girls will remember (her, their) work tomorrow.
3. Mary and Joan directed (her, their) groups well, but neither Margaret nor Pat seemed to be able to keep (hers, theirs) on schedule.
4. Nobody believed what (he, they) heard when the President answered the reporter's question.
5. Everybody said (he, they) had expected the President to deny the charges against his aide.
6. Another of the women asked to change (her, their) job today.
7. When Hae Sung or her roommate sees what you've done, (she, they) will want to rearrange the room.
8. If someone calls for Adriana, tell (him, them) that she will be in a meeting until noon.
9. One of the girls tried to use (her, their) influence to change the date of the meeting.
10. Anyone else from the group would have been afraid to admit (his, their) part in the plot.

11.　Everybody can help (himself, themselves) to the dessert that's left.

12.　When no one reached for (his, their) money, Helen paid the check.

13.　Either Dennis or Heng will bring (his, their) truck to help you move.

14.　Anyone who has made (his, their) choice can come to the front to pick up (his, their) selection.

15.　Will everyone be able to find (his, their) way back to the campsite?

B.　Correct errors in pronoun agreement in the sentences below.

1.　What this play needs is someone who can remember their lines.

2.　Neither the star nor the other actors knew his lines at the rehearsal last week.

3.　I hope everyone knows their part before the director arrives today.

4.　If anyone asks where I've gone, tell them to mind their own business.

5.　Each of the workmen has put their tools away for the day.

6.　After Ed and Phil decided on the changes, each went away to work on their own.

7.　Another of the children went home today because they felt sick.

8.　Janet and Teresita knew that her work would be checked, but neither of the women bothered to check their own work first.

9.　Do you think either Rose or her sister can find their way home?

10.　Neither of the vocalists sang their best.

CHAPTER 36

Passive Voice

Ever wonder why you have trouble reading something even though you know all the words? Perhaps you're struggling through sentence after sentence of passive voice. Like most readers you've come to expect sentences in the active voice, although you may not know what active and passive mean.

The natural order for an English sentence—actor-action-acted upon—requires *active voice,* as in the following:

> *Jonathan*   *ate*   the *doughnut.*
> (actor)   (action)   (acted upon)

Notice that the subject of the sentence is the actor (the one doing the eating).

You risk distracting or annoying your reader with passive voice because it reverses this normal, expected order. Instead, the subject changes: it is no longer the actor. The new subject is acted upon, as in this *passive voice* sentence:

> The *doughnut*   *was eaten*   by *Jonathan.*
> (acted upon)   (action)   (actor)

Notice that the actor now appears in a phrase after the verb. However, the passive sentence may not even name the actor, as in this version:

> The *doughnut was eaten.*
> (acted upon)   (action)

A simple comparison of the active and passive sentences above allows us to see the disadvantages of the passive voice: (1) passive constructions are more wordy than active constructions; (2) because passive voice reverses the normal sentence order, passive constructions are indirect; (3) as the name "passive" implies, passive constructions lack the vigor inherent in active verbs; and (4) if the writer forgets to tell us who the actor is, the passive construction is vague. For these reasons, active voice is better than passive, suggesting a simple rule for you to follow: write with the active voice unless you have an excellent reason for using the passive.

RECOGNIZING PASSIVE VOICE

Students often complain that they cannot tell whether a verb is active or passive, but identification is really quite simple. Only a passive sentence will receive "yes" answers in all of the following tests:

    1. Is the subject of the sentence *acted upon*? In our sample passive sentence, *doughnut*, the subject of the sentence, is acted upon (eaten) by Jonathan.

    2. Does the sentence use a form of the verb *to be* followed by the kind of main verb that almost always ends in *-ed* or *-en*? The simple forms of *to be* are these: *is, am, are, was,* and *were*. Compound forms of *to be* use *be, being,* or *been* (for example, *will be, is being, has been*). Thus, passive verbs look like these: *is divided, was beaten,* and *will have been destroyed*. In our sample passive sentence, *was eaten* is the passive verb form.

    3. If the actor appears in the sentence, is the actor in the prepositional phrase "by someone or something"? If the actor is not given, does the sense of the sentence imply "by someone or something"? "The doughnut was eaten by Jonathan" ends with *by Jonathan*, whereas "The doughnut was eaten" implies "by someone."

USING PASSIVE VOICE

You may have decided by now that the passive voice was created (by someone) merely to entrap you. Not so. In fact, passive constructions do have legitimate uses:

    1. Passive voice is useful when the object of the action is more important than the actor:

> Residents of Sandstone, Nevada, are afraid that a lethal gas manufactured in nearby Cactus Flower may someday poison them. They fear, for example, that the lethal gas *may be released* by a defective valve or a worn gasket.

The emphasis in the last sentence is clearly on the lethal gas. That is, the context of the passage makes the gas more important than the parts that might allow a leak. Only passive voice will allow the object of the action (lethal gas) to gain emphasis by appearing first in the sentence.

2. Because passive voice can hide the actor, it is useful when the actor is obvious, unimportant, or uncertain. For example, if we did not know who dropped a canister of gas, we might write this:

> When a canister *was dropped*, a lethal gas enveloped the laboratory workers.

However, a strong warning is necessary here: the worst misuse of passive voice occurs when the reader wants or needs to know who the actor is and the writer doesn't bother to say. Imagine being told this:

> Leave your application in the box. If you *are found* acceptable, you *will be notified.*

Because you want to know who will judge you, or at least who will notify you, the omission of the actors is very irritating.

Deciding when the rules apply requires good judgment. If you try hard enough to convince yourself, you can stretch these justifications for passive voice to cover most sentences. Therefore, keep in mind the general rule: use the passive voice only when you have a strong reason.

ACTIVATING THE PASSIVE

Far too often students use passive voice because they can't think how to write the sentence in the active voice; in such cases the passive is more accidental than intentional. You can prevent this lack of control in your own writing by learning the following three methods to convert passive voice into active:

1. Reverse the object and the subject.
    Passive: An example *is shown* in Figure 3.
    Active: Figure 3 *shows* an example.
2. Delete the main verb, leaving the sentence with a form of *to be* as the only verb.
    Passive: Your cousin *is seen* as the best candidate.
    Active: Your cousin *is* the best candidate.
3. Change the verb.
    Passive: Jonathan *was given* a new book.
    Active: Jonathan *received* a new book.

If you learn to recognize the passive voice and determine to avoid the passive whenever you can, these three methods will provide you the tools you need to write simple, direct, and vigorous active sentences.

EXERCISES

A. Explain the three tests that identify passive voice.

1. _____

_____

2. _____

_____

3. _____

_____

B. Name the two justifications for using passive voice.

1. _____

_____

2. _____

_____

C. Write the three methods for changing passive voice to active voice.

1. _____

_____

2. _____

_____

3. _____

_____

D. Rewrite the following sentences to eliminate all passive voice. When necessary, supply the actors.

1. Janet's proposal is seen as the best of the options.
2. The merit of her proposal is evidenced by the cost and benefit statistics she provided.
3. The motion to censure the Congressman will be considered by the full House tomorrow.
4. The pickpocket was seized when he tried to use a stolen credit card.

5. The pencil shaft is made of wood.

6. A note was left on the window of the car by the man who ran into it.

7. When work on the patio is finished, we will plant azaleas around the edges.

8. Before the local television station ran the movie, three of the scenes were edited out of it.

9. Once the cylinder has been set on the platform, be sure not to jiggle it.

10. The fertilizer was spread by Ken.

11. Once the horse race is started, you will not be able to place a bet.

12. The small gray mouse was chased around the room by the cat.

13. If the bell is rung on schedule, I'll have time to catch my bus.

14. Martha's house is located in Cleveland.

15. The wagon was fixed by Kim's brother.

CHAPTER 37

Word Choice

The French have a phrase that could be the title of this chapter (but who reads French?). The phrase is *le mot juste,* and it means—roughly—"the right word." *Le mot juste* is often the difference between an A paper and a merely ordinary C paper—not just one good word, of course, but a lot of them. This chapter covers some basic and advanced techniques for finding those good words.

BASIC TECHNIQUES

What is a good word? Is it something really impressive, a big word that proves how educated we are? No. Usually it's a word we all know. Unfortunately—even though it's a common word—we don't use it very often because another more general word is even more common. *See* is one of those more general words we might slap down on a rough draft, but think of all the synonyms that might work better: *glimpse, gaze, stare, peer, spot,* or *witness.*

Let's take a longer example. Suppose you are reading a paragraph and run across these words:

The man walked into the room.

The words are so general they could fit into a number of strikingly different contexts:

The policeman, hidden behind a parked car, watched as *the man walked into the room.*

OR

The Capitol guard smiled as *the man walked into the room.*

OR

The class quieted somewhat as *the man walked into the room.*

OR

The patients gasped as *the man walked into the room.*

"What a great clause!" you say. "I can use it anywhere." It's a lousy clause—you can use it anywhere. All the words are general, the kind of words that pop into your mind in a second. Let's think a second longer and try to make the words more exact. Here are some possibilities:

Man: thief, senator, English teacher, Dr. Rodney

Walked: sneaked, hurried, sauntered, reeled

Room: motel room, antechamber, classroom, office

Now let's rewrite that all-purpose bad clause using more specific words:

The policeman, hidden behind a parked car, watched as *the thief sneaked into my motel room.*

OR

The Capitol guard smiled as the *senator hurried into the antechamber.*

OR

The class quieted somewhat as *the English teacher sauntered into the classroom.*

OR

The patients gasped as *Dr. Rodney reeled into his office.*

Each clause is better—and certainly more interesting—because the writer took the time to come up with just the right words. Try it yourself. Look for those dull, general words in your own writing and make them more specific. This technique is one of the best ways to improve your writing dramatically.

Let's take a moment for a warning, though. Don't become so obsessed with the idea of seeking different words that you choose unusual ones. *Perambulate,* for example, means "to walk through," so we could write this sentence:

The senator perambulated the antechamber.

The reader will probably notice the peculiarity of *perambulated* rather than its preciseness. Your goal is getting the right word, not the unusual word.

The second basic technique, in addition to using the right word, is to use modifiers. Sometimes the nouns and verbs don't tell the whole story.

To be really precise, you need to add some adjectives and adverbs. Let's work with one of the sentences we improved in the last section:

> The policeman, hidden behind a parked car, watched as the thief sneaked into my motel room.

From the clause we revised ("the thief sneaked into my motel room"), we can modify *thief, sneaked,* and *motel room.* Here are just a few possibilities:

We don't want to overload the sentence with modifiers, so let's just modify *thief* and *sneaked:*

> The policeman, hidden behind a parked car, watched as the shifty-eyed thief sneaked noiselessly into my motel room.

We've come a long way from "The man walked into the room," haven't we?

Again, a warning: don't get so carried away that you pile up modifier after modifier. Only the writer and his mother could love this sentence:

> The dimunitive, chunky, azure-eyed, eighteen-month-old boy toddled to his rocking horse.

ADVANCED TECHNIQUES

If you really want to get your reader's attention, use a comparison. It may be the most memorable part of your theme. Remember when we said transitions are like road signs? And when we said the blueprint for your paper is like the architect's design for the structure he plans to build? These and other comparisons really help your reader understand an idea.

Only one problem with comparisons: they're hard to think of, particularly good comparisons. We can all think of bad ones. The familiar phrases that come to mind almost automatically are clichés, and they are as bad as original comparisons are good. Consider this sentence:

> Although he was *blind as a bat*, Herman remained *cool as a cucumber* when he entered the arena.

See how clichés attract the wrong kind of attention to themselves? Hearing a cliché is like hearing a comedian go through the same routine time after time. After a while, nobody listens.

A good rule is that if you have heard a comparison before, don't use it. But do use original comparisons. Be daring. Try one on your next theme.

Here's something else to try on your next theme: when you want to use a general word that stands for an entire class of items—like *toys* or *vehicles* or *books*—use just one item from that class instead. Let the specific stand for the general. Take this sentence:

> Inflation means that most Americans can hardly afford to eat, but some congressmen don't seem to care how much *food* costs.

Let's make the sentence a little more interesting by replacing the word *food* (an entire class of items) with *a loaf of bread* (one item from that class):

> Inflation means that most Americans can hardly afford to eat, but some congressmen don't seem to care how much *a loaf of bread* costs.

Here's another example:

> As a photographer he is limited. He may be able to take pictures of *nature*, but he can't take good pictures of people.

We can make the second sentence more interesting by changing the word *nature* to something more specific:

> As a photographer he is limited. He may be able to take pictures of *trees*, but he can't take good pictures of people.

See how the detail instead of the generality makes the sentence livelier?

Most college students don't use either of the advanced techniques in this section. Most of them don't get A's either. If you want to learn how to write an A paper, you might start by occasionally using a comparison or a specific word instead of a general one.

EXERCISES

A. Rewrite the following sentences two different ways, replacing the underlined general words with more precise words.

> Example: The official talked to the man.
>   a.   The district attorney grilled the arsonist.
>   b.   The manager congratulated the pitcher.

1. The speaker showed his evidence.

    a. _____

    b. _____
2. The animal ate the food.

    a. _____

    b. _____
3. The people liked the plant.

    a. _____

    b. _____
4. The woman disliked the furniture.

    a. _____

    b. _____
5. The scientist talked about his invention.

    a. _____

    b. _____

B. In each sentence below, write a modifier in the blank. Make the modifier as colorful and specific as you can. Try to fit it to the context.

> Example: The _____ policeman arrested the mayor.

Words like *short* and *young* may not help much. On the other hand, try these choices:

The *rookie* policeman arrested the mayor.

OR

The *bitter* policeman arrested the mayor.

1. The _____ tiger stalked the gazelle.
2. The _____ pilot winced when the plane hit the air turbulence.
3. The _____ carpet startled the new owner.
4. The gardener was very surprised to find such a/an _____ bug on the end of his shovel.
5. The _____ actor used to be familiar to everyone in this town.
6. My first year in college is a/an _____ experience.
7. As the _____ safecracker gently touched the dial, the telephone suddenly rang.
8. I don't see how anybody can read this _____ map!
9. The _____ town was just as he had imagined it.
10. The _____ criminal fled to the Everglades.

C. We use comparisons every day, but too many of them are clichés, like "nervous as a cat on a hot tin roof" or "scared as a rabbit." For this exercise write one original comparison on any topic. (If you have trouble thinking of a topic, consider blind dates, a hobby, a famous person.)

_____

_____

_____

_____

D. List three clichés other than the ones we've used as examples. (Remember, clichés are bad. Avoid them like the plague.)

1. _____

2. _____

3. _____

E. Improve the sentences below by changing each italicized generalization to something more specific.

> Example: Small movie houses that show film classics are going out of business. After all, who wants to pay *good money* to see *an old movie*?

Revision: Small movie houses that show film classics are
going out of business. After all, who wants to pay
three dollars to see *Humphrey Bogart?*

1. Public television advocates claim that viewers today are at-
tracted to mindless programs, spending all their time watching *situation comedies* and *sports.*

situation comedies: _____

sports: _____

2. *Not too long ago, grade-school students* didn't know how to
use *basic punctuation marks.*

Not too long ago: _____

grade-school students: _____

basic punctuation marks: _____

appendix

Theme Format

Incredible as it may seem, English teachers are just like you and me (well —maybe a little more like me). Like you, they're human and have their little eccentricities. For example, they think that if students have done a good job writing their themes, they'll also want to make them as neat as possible. Silly idea—or is it?

That idea also has its corollary: the student who writes a theme at the last minute probably doesn't take—doesn't even *have*—the time to make it neat.

The moral is clear: be neat so that your instructor thinks he's looking at an A paper before he's read even the first word. Here are some guidelines, although your instructor may wish to make some changes to suit individual preferences.

Handwriting or Typing?   Look at the two sample papers that follow. Which one would you rather read? If you can type at all, then do so. The early papers are short enough that typing them should not take very long.

If you don't type, use either black or blue ink. Other colors are hard to read.

Proofreading   Do it—always, but especially if you type. Otherwise, you might be surprised what your magic fingers did the night before.

Paper   If you type, use standard-sized (8½'' by 11'') typing paper. The erasable kind is especially good because you can make corrections easily. The thin "onionskin" typing paper is hard for your instructor to write on because it absorbs ink quickly. Don't use it.

If you don't type, find a standard-sized tablet of high-quality, lined theme paper. But don't use ordinary notebook paper (or paper torn from a spiral notebook) unless your instructor approves.

Corrections   On a short paper (like the one-paragraph essay), avoid handing in a paper with obvious corrections. If, however, you're torn between making a correction at the last minute or handing in a neat paper, of course make the correction. What good is a neat error?

Spacing   If you're typing, double-space. If not, write on every other line.

Margins   Allow an inch on the top (except page one), left, right, and bottom. On page one, center your title two inches from the top, then triple-space to start your theme.

Page numbers   Don't number page one. For the other pages, put the number in the upper right-hand corner.

Identification   Put your name, course number, instructor's name, and date in the upper right-hand corner of page one.

Fastening the Paper   Use a stapler. Paper clips are fine in theory, but in a stack of themes they tend to clip themselves onto other themes.

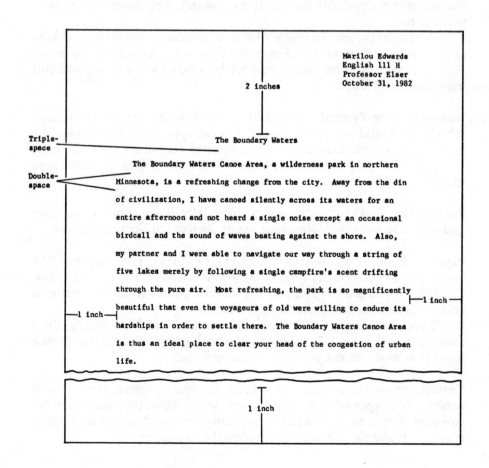

Marilou Edwards
English 111 H
Professor Elser
October 31, 1982

The Boundary Waters

The Boundary Waters Canoe Area, a wilderness park in northern Minnesota, is a refreshing change from the city. Away from the din of civilization, I have canoed silently across its waters for an entire afternoon and not heard a single noise except an occasional birdcall and the sound of the waves beating against the shore. Also, my partner and I were able to navigate our way through a string of five lakes merely by following a single campfire's scent drifting through the pure air. Most refreshing, the park is so magnificently beautiful that even the voyageurs of old were willing to endure its hardships in order to settle there. The Boundary Waters Canoe Area is thus an ideal place to clear your head of the congestion of urban life.

Index